TRIBUTE

To each mountain goat and camel who walked with me during this ten year writer's marathon. My goats have climbed pinnacles with me. The camels have shouldered burdens in personal deserts. A few of you have been both camel and goat. I'm eternally grateful for your celebration and sweat equity. I love you on both sides of heaven. Christina

To my Mom who I believe is reading this from heaven. She'd see this book finally published and repeat, "Oh Wow! Oh! Wow!" as she almost reverently turned each page. She'd pause long enough between wows to excitedly tell my Dad, "Oh Bob! Go get the camera! We need to get a picture of this." She'd tell me, "You done your mama proud." Mom with tears filled with lessons and blessin's, "Shersie Bug."

LIFE'S TOO SHORT FOR DULL RAZORS, CHEAP PENS, AND WORN OUT UNDERWEAR

By Christina Eder

Copyright © 2019 by Christina Eder

Behind the scenes. An intriguing insight. A historical hindsight.

Q *(as asked by innocent bystanders): Why don't you write a book?*

A *(as answered by the person writing this book/sitting in this chair/typing this manuscript/Christina Eder): I don't know.*

Q: *How do you come up with all these random comments?*

A: *I just think while I run.*

Statement *(invitation stemmed from random conversations): You should write a book.*

Response *(answered in question format after said random conversations): Doesn't everyone suggest the book writing scene to someone after one semi-intelligent sentence?*

Statement: *Yeah, but your stuff is funny and most people won't say the things you say out loud anymore.*

Response: *Maybe they're the smart ones and I could follow their example of keeping my mouth shut more of the time.*

Statement: *But that would be boring.*

Response: *Boring is safer and more sanitary.*

Challenge: *Don't settle for boring. I dare you. No! I double dog dare you to write all this down!*

This is officially the first sentence of a book that sojourners on this side of heaven have suggested, prodded, and recently double-dog dared me to write. I have no clue where this will go. I've published magazine articles, written for newspapers, and authored various columns. My best friend since third grade has been a diary, which we've graduated to the more adult reference, journal. Those short, smaller, more private pieces are within my semi-comfortable reach, but writing an entire book?

Like golf or knitting, writing a book seems to be a modern hobby or trendy outlet. How do my thoughts vary from billions of published books or Facebook postings? Do I even have enough material or tenacity to complete a book?

I write this for the friend who used my own coach-to-courageous quip when she issued this double-dog dare: "Put your spleen out there on the chopping block. What have you got to lose?" For an audience of two, possibly three including an editor, I rise to this literary challenge.

With over four decades of earthly street cred, a few years as a "newspaper geek," and thousands of running miles to think, I write this book. It is a (out of the) box set of humor and random musings that few people discuss, but possibly wonder. Perhaps I write these musings wondering if other people wonder. It is a collection of mountain top joys that need to be birthed simply for recalling delicious bites of my life. This book houses examples of my sometimes compromised values that left me with a lesson only after face planting in deserts.

Through thick and thin, ebbs and flows, peaks and valleys, crunchy and creamy, plastic or paper, I offer only one conclusion. Life's too short for dull razors, cheap pens, and worn-out underwear.

A FEW MISUNDERSTANDINGS AND A LOT OF UNDEFINED ANSWERS

"I know you like running, but if you don't use headphones or listen to music while you run, what do you think about during all that time?"

When I explain how I combine fitness running with treasured think time, a version of this question follows: "What could possibly fill your mind to pass the time after running the first one or two miles?

Other running related curiosities include how many miles I run each week; what brand of shoes I wear; how do I recover from various body pains; am I afraid of skunks on trail runs; why do I get up before 6:00 in the morning 'just' to run; do I carry pepper spray. The winner of *The Most Frequently Asked Question For Loving Distance Running on a Voluntary Basis* award goes to...: "What in the heck can you ponder to keep you running for all that time without going nuts?"

I could end this book here. "Everything. Nothing. You name it. What *don't* I think about when I run?" This written journey invites me to answer that question with personal transparency. I started this book in 2008 shortly before our son graduated from high school. It's July 2018. Two weeks ago I finished this ten year compilation and it's time to begin the tedious editing process. Pieces of this "soul X-ray" will stay and pieces will be scrapped. Some reflections were birthed after laborious running miles in the sun. A few topics originated during Midwest winters when I ran a bob-and-weave-pattern-to-try-to-stay-warm-as-I-dodged-frozen-cow-pies.

Instead of a Once Upon a Time beginning, I'm inserting a virtual auditory harp interlude here. You know that finger glide over harp strings just as the TV actor falls asleep and begins dreaming? For full effect, I'm mentally adding a wavy screen and picture fade out while said harp music plays…

When I first began running, crop tops were "in," but my teen gut was protruding a little. I didn't necessarily have a weight problem, but I did carry some extra gravitational pull on the earth that needed toning. In addition to cutting out whole milk and ice cream, I incorporated the E word (exercise, not eggplant). Many girls my age were on volleyball and basketball teams. When it came to ball sports, I was afraid the flying orb would break my glasses. No matter how many times I heard, "keep your eye on the ball," when any object was thrown within a six block radius of me, I struck a pose similar to a cat being put in a bathtub. During gym class, I silently prayed the ball *wouldn't* get thrown to me.

Despite these concerns, I looked for a cardio activity that would work various muscle groups and require minimal hand-eye coordination. I did not want to learn numerous game rules or invest money and storage space for special equipment. Given those criteria, running became my best option. Good shoes, inhale, exhale, left foot, right foot, repeat many, many, many times. Generally speaking, I was, and still am disciplined, so I didn't require a drill sergeant, sports team, or gym membership to nurture my fitness goals.

I started a training pattern of alternately walking 100 steps, running 100 steps until I was out of breath. Those 15 minutes each day for the first week weren't a large investment of time and quickly progressing baby steps motivated me. When I needed a push, I'd remind myself: "C'mon, when you complete this 15 minute run today, you'll still have a free 23 ¾ hours left. You've got this!" Each Friday, I decreased the walking steps by 10 and continued running 100 steps so recovery time between walking and running was less. After a couple of weeks of running 15-minute bursts, I may have sounded like some exercise infomercial. I was sleeping better, gaining energy and mental alertness, increasing strength, less out of breath and juggling flaming torches from the third story balcony. Oh wait. Exaggeration on the infomercial. Juggling more than a schedule involves that hand-eye coordination thing I intentionally avoid.

I enjoyed the perks of committed exercise. My next focus was to develop a more consistent running stride. I synchronized my pace to the Old McDonald Had a Farm song. When running I only sang this catchy little farm lilt in my head, not at the top of my lungs. Periodically pacing myself to the timing Old

McDonald freed me from complicating the running experience with gauges, pedometers, watches, wires, or headphones. I embrace the age of tech*no* (emphasis on the *no)* to eliminate extra gadgets. After thirty-plus years of running, Old McDonald is still my musical pace car though sometimes my stride indicates that Old McDonald's tractor needs an overhaul, pigs are dwindling from hunger, and ducks sure could use an updraft to get them off the ground.

To increase my running endurance, I added time and distance every Friday. It became a personal challenge to see how far I could stretch myself. My stamina began with increased physical strength followed by mental tenacity. Ultimately running built a spiritual foundation, although at 13 years old, I had no intention of exploring divine evolution. I was physically toning up and gaining inner confidence that stemmed from pushing *to* a challenge then *through* a challenge.

I unveil the following snapshots as part of a "written photo album" that spans through various mind travels. This collage weaves word art into frames of my running trail dialogue.

CONFESSION

When I originally started writing this book, my purpose was to create a collection of transparent thoughts harvested from seeds of three decades of running. I wanted to portray that a sense of humor and optimism is key to running perseverance.

The written potpourri was intended to be lighthearted and comical, sometimes filled with random silliness. A few trusted people read my first drafts and graciously guided me away from my undertone of jaded flippancy. These mercifully honest people told me the book read more demeaning and preachy. They expected my natural default to sprinkle upbeat wit into everyday situations to show up on the pages. Instead, they were met with disappointment that I wrote something that was dramatically different than who I really am when they're around. Ouch. My heart took a sucker punch because a lot of these people have known me for much of my life.

My knee-jerk reaction instantly licked my wounds. If I was going to write a book, I wanted it to have power, to stand out with a message deeper than something they'd read on the back of a furniture polish bottle. My mission in writing a book wasn't to portray myself as a cynical broom rider with frequent flier miles on her sweeper. My next line of defense, saturated in defensiveness, was some people reading my manuscript had *obviously* gotten stuffy over the years since we've known each other. Maybe they no longer "got" my random sense of humor.

I felt too exposed, too volatile, too embarrassed to fight back. Those first drafts required significant sweat equity. I thought I had thicker skin and more willing to accept constructive input. Had I intersected the fine lines between quick wit, sarcasm, and cynicism? In a wearied state, I let the book sit for over two years. Fast forwarding through a litany of internal dialogue, lengthy journal entries, and a few hundred days of living the earthly experience, I received a "wider lens" perspective. After two years of manuscript dormancy, I pulled the most recent version of my book from a stack of papers. I read comments and editor remarks through a lighter filter. I read through a filter that didn't promote fire and brimstone pulpits. I studied through a filter that didn't accept lack of compassion. Yikes.

Thankfully, I was gently convicted enough to admit that instead of what I originally thought was refreshing transparency was raw, unbecoming cynicism. I used a written platform to mask personal unresolved issues that bit with a "get-back-at-the-world" bitter spirit. I'm eternally grateful for those people who exposed this edgy truth with loving honesty.

In my original drafts, I covered up this unexplored section of my soul, fearing that readers would think I was too "out there." Over years of running, I have accumulated fresh insights and discovered an intensely spiritual side I had not expected or sought. So, with sincere appreciation to my writing life coach who encouraged me to dig beyond "see" level, I write this unplugged, more healed version of my running thoughts.

TUBE SOCKS, CROP TOPS, AND DRAWSTRING SWEATPANTS

I began running in the early 80's when trendy clothing statements included three-band colored tube socks, rainbow half shirts, and baggie hip hugger sweatpants with elastic cuffs at the bottom. Looking back at those photos, I burst into a sauna sweat. It's horribly clear to me why I could run in the dark without ever being attacked. That crude mix of a crop top, ballooning sweatpants and sweaty Aqua net plastered to my skull like a swim cap supersedes any black belt self-defense course.

Being a rookie runner, my predominant thoughts were not about what clothes I'd wear. I concentrated on running form alignment, breathing for maximum lung capacity, increasing distance, and quickening my speed. Especially on higher traffic roads, I wanted to avoid a basset hound running stance. Sauntering like a basset hound is most certainly not a put down to the canine community. Anyone who has spent time with me points out that I acknowledge the dog long before I realize there's even a person belonging to the dog.

I easily remember a dog's name but find myself asking the human at the end of their dog's leash to reintroduce themselves. There's an outbreak of owners walking their dog while checking their cell phones so I appreciate that the dog notices me before their human does. Fido and I prefer old fashioned wireless communication.

Oops! I digress. I see incorporating dogs into any story as windows of conversational opportunity.

Back to crop top running.

I'm thankful for growing up when crop tops were stylish, mostly because those undersized shirts encouraged me to keep my ab muscles sucked in tight. I also vote for a less publicized but highly effective method to maintain rock solid abs. The Double-Up-Laughter Workout, created by designers of those dang 80's style drawstring sweatpants, were onto something when they crafted that moody drawstring. Tying, untying, and retying that ornery noose was merely a warm-up for what wardrobe catastrophe that was bound to happen. Tied too loose, I risked less-than-aerodynamic strides in tugging and hiking up those balloon bottom bubble britches. Tied too tight, I lost oxygen flow and ran the risk of passing out, which significantly decreases running mileage and lessens the odds of personal record that day.

Back to drawstrings…the double knot tie best compensated for movement without dropping my drawers. The hazard in that double knot strategy threw me into immediate danger during post-running bathroom breaks. During those red alert rest stops there were more times than I care to recall where I thought I had the *perfect* double knot tension, only to back up to the toilet and find that perfection went south! If you have ever collided with this knot-in-the-drawstring-and-I-have-to-go-to-the-bathroom-so-bad-I'm-ready-to-hurl tragedy, you already know this twisted ending.

Imagine the endorphins releasing, toxins are purging, muscles pulsating, and feet that are oh so ready to kick off shoes you've been running in for miles. You grab a cold glass of water and eagerly traipse to the bathroom to rid your bladder of all pre-workout hydration. You pull the right side of the drawstring tail as you take long stride glides to the bathroom. You shuffle quickly to the toilet, quickly pulling the other string to unleash your masterly tied knot. You grab the knot at the base and pull it forward, using the fingernail on your other hand to free the tie. Miles ago this double knot was the perfect fastener. Miles later, after sweat coupled with swollen fingers, you must activate your cleverness. Sticking your hip way out to one side, you pull at the knot base once again, this time sucking in your stomach for more maneuvering room. Sucking in your stomach with a full bladder is nothing short of a half marathon by itself.

You feverishly tell yourself to chill out. Working yourself into a coronary isn't going to deliver you from this drawstring bondage any sooner. You will yourself not to allow one knotted string in a waistband to increase your blood pressure. If kidneys could talk, they are screaming, "Enough already!

Hurry up oh mighty warrior runner!" You break a post-workout sweat brought on by sheer frustration. You take shallow cleansings breath to re-center yourself for this immediate rescue mission at hand. You wipe sweat from your hands and try a sharper fingernail to loosen that drawstring. You may be desperate enough to cross-legged shuffle-jog to the kitchen for a fork prong to dislodge the knot. Heightened creativity ensues. The only heat-of-the-moment-solution appears to be pulling up any excessive sweatpants material you can bundle at the waist and bending over far enough to get your teeth to the knot and bite out the knot. Somehow, you finally come to your senses, seek out the closest pair of scissors, and snip the knot away from the shackle. Thankfully, more practical workout bottoms have replaced the 80's ripcord fashion and that drawstring sweatpants trend is knot in style.

A WAVE RUNNER

I'm fascinated by watching someone's response when I smile or wave at them along my running route. Some people tentatively wave back with a facial expression that indicates they'll spend the next minutes figuring out how or even if they know. Other people give a polite but hesitant mirrored image and return a smile. The majority of people respond with appreciation and their body language conveys uplift when they wave back.

Those welcomed reactions inspire me to see how many more smiles I can generate from other drivers, bikers, or walkers as we pass each other. Similar to a running mileage goal, I set a smiling goal. Although I'm unable to forecast the number of travelers on my running route, I *can* set a quota for sharing a smile or wave with each person I pass. If I look like I'm desperately hailing a cab during rush hour, I'm probably way below my wave and smile quota that day.

As with any objective, sometimes the original target needs finer tuning. For example, on rainy days, with typically fewer foot travelers, wave and smile collections lessen. On sunny days, more people are enjoying the outdoor activities so smile and wave numbers drastically increase. This hypothesis will probably not generate a scientific theory, but measuring waves and smiles adds entertainment when my brighter outlook wanes toward the running finish line. I see running as a potential cheering ministry. I'd wager a guess that many people appreciate someone acknowledging their presence with at least a quick friendly interchange. Extended eye contact or an invitation to stop mid-run to chat negates a lot of my cheer. The key word here is *quick* interchange.

Not everyone returns basic acknowledgement. Sometimes, people scowl or appear oblivious that another person is directly in their path. Just as a farmer doesn't expect one planted seed to produce a bumper crop harvest, I try not to let a few unpleasant "weeds" rain on my smile parade. If there aren't weeds, I have no comparison for welcoming bright flowers.

Reciprocated waves, smiles, and hellos far outweigh the negative or blank expressions. To challenge both mind and body, I created a mental cross training version of my smile and wave game. It's a self-guided betting game to see how often I can get their response correct.

For example, when a car or person is coming down the street, I wager a guess about how that particular foot traveler or driver will react to my wave or smile. Since I'm betting against myself, this drastically reduces the suspense of who will win the non-existent jackpot. The categories include, but are not limited to:

1. Returned smile

2. Reciprocal wave
3. Questioning eyebrow raise
4. Complete disregard
5. Unwelcomed scowl

When I guess a passerby's response correctly, I give myself an internal cheer. When I vote inaccurately, my game show voice takes over to create a sometimes obnoxious, but non-catastrophic reason for misreading a reaction. The guessing game goes a little like this (it may add a special effect to import your best game show host voice here): "Christina! You guessed the driver in that fancy SUV would wave, with hopes that a smile would follow. However, due to this driver's prior circumstances, you won her full-house poker face! You assumed she was returning from a fancy tea party, filled with make-me-happy food and friendly interactions. You couldn't fathom that you'd receive less than a liberal smile/wave combo. Instead, Christina, our dear but assumptive contestant, here is a walk-a-mile-in-her heels perspective: Driver X just left a cut-rate salon and went toe-to-toe with perhaps the worst pedicure of her life. With foot crunches that cramped her style, she gingerly shuffled to the salon parking lot on the outside of her heels to avoid dismantling those flimsy spa slippers. As she stares at her toenails, she is horrified that the burnt sienna color looked extensively more muted in the bottle. Post-pedicure, Driver X is subjected to facing ten neon-orange pedal digits for days and days. So Christina, let's offer this traumatized driver a daily double card from your grace and mercy deck. Let's have our next traveling contestant on *My Guess Could be Right!*"

In addition to the five primary response categories mentioned above, I include a bonus round for special occasions. This extended game version is saved for endurance runs. It's like a box set edition of *My Guess Could be Right,* challenging not only a person's response, but stakes how many people mirror my waving style. I use the same unwritten guidelines for returning my hello but verbal acknowledgement applies only to foot traffic, not people in vehicles.

I experiment with assorted waves to see if a person reflects the same style. I try the fancy wave where I mostly wiggle the top 4 fingers, sometimes tucking the thumb to wiggle for a special cameo appearance to support the other 4 cast members. Since it's difficult for me to wiggle my thumb, I reserve this wave for the warm-up mile before blood pumps heaviest to my fingers.

There's a simple palm raise without much waving motion; the back and forth wave; the over-the-head-afterthought wave that happens when more than one traveler passes. I have heightened respect for Wal-Mart greeters who are fluent in multiple salutations when massive amounts of shoppers enter the store front. I prefer focusing on the one-on-one smile and wave.

After many miles of 'scientifically' tracking waves, I've discovered my default wave is holding my pointer finger and pinky as bookends and then bringing the other two fingers toward my palm with three quick repetitive motions downward. My semi-bent thumb holds moderately still while the other four fingers do the wave stance. I pause for a chair break because I've simultaneously written this paragraph formulating words that match the wave. Ironically, I'm more concerned about accurately painting a visual picture for the reader than someone walking past my office as I flail my hands and quietly mumble words while featuring an assortment of facial expressions in front of the computer screen.

Back to greeting people on my running route…

Timing, eye contact, and body language are keys in estimating a person's response. Verbal acknowledgement adds a bonus round challenge to the game total. A wave, smile, *and* hello become a package deal. Sometimes it's simply making the best choice between one of the three options to avoid overwhelming an innocent sojourner.

Most of the time, my gut instinct is to initiate that pointer finger, pinky as bookends wave as stated above. If the person waves back, I add a smile. Depending on how winded I am from my run, I sometimes add a hello. A word of caution: if I'm winded and try to breathe out a hello, this well-intended greeting sounds more like a midnight call-in ad featuring a long phone number that charges upwards of $1.99 per minute.

Timing is vital. If I verbally acknowledge someone from a substantial distance, I resemble a two-year-old hailing everyone in a ½ block radius. A gregarious hi from a toddler often generates laughter and the general population defines these repetitive hellos cute. However, an adult prematurely beckoning hello lends itself to social awkwardness.

What about eye contact guidelines? At what distance do I glance at an upcoming trail blazer and how do I maintain gentle eye contact that differs from a stare-down? There must be some ancient facial dance that ensues between two people who make eye contact from yards away. That distance gap becomes an eye tango until those two people physically reach each other. For instance: Person A sees Person B approaching from a 150 yards distance. It's too early to say hello so Person A smiles just as Person B looks down. Person B doesn't see Person A's initial connection. Person B moves head back to upright position and smiles at Person A. Person A misses Person B's delayed smile because Person A changes focus from Person B to surrounding scenery. Person B follows Person A's eye dance lead to look at scenery. Variations of this facial foxtrot ensue until finally the eye dancers bridge the gap and exchange pleasantries.

However personal connections are created, if I have shared abundant waves and smiles, it's a fruitful running day. My life mission to encourage all people in my path grows stronger as my physical endurance becomes more solid.

WORDS COUNT

One thing I discovered from greeting people while I ran was a growing desire to be more compassionate. I found myself more willing to reach out to needy and hurting people. I wanted to support and encourage others without fear they would reject me or my help. I wondered what would happen if I began talking to God about people, current events, and social justice topics that entered my mind while I ran. Since I was already thinking I might as well use that head space to ask God about these often disturbing situations.

As a baby Christian, my prayer process started out (gulp) testing God's faithfulness. I yearned to distinguish between His guidance and my own immature quick solution. I wanted two-way communication with Him much like I do with any other person. One talks, one responds, alternate, repeat. I naively figured that conversation method worked with God also.

I was raised in a strong Christian home. We said meal prayers and bedtime prayers. We went to church every Sunday and I still had many questions and concerns about prayer. What in the heck was I supposed to do when I asked God something or told Him something and He didn't answer? Did I do something wrong? What happens when I don't know if an answer was my own idea or if the solution really was from God? Was I not listening hard enough?

Did I misread an invitation to connect with God on a new level? Was I supposed to feel something every time I prayed? Would I hear from God each day? Who could I talk to about this? Who could I trust to not judge me as wacky? Who would give me a truthful answer instead of the generic "you'll just know" response?

I needed clarity from someone who was more spiritually advanced, someone further along on their spiritual journey. As a woman in my late teens I didn't have confidence to broach this subject with anyone. That act of courage would have been like putting my spleen out on the chopping block!

I decided instead of seeking human insight, I'd keep talking to God (in my head) as I ran each morning. I'd listen more intently for His input. Even though God doesn't weigh prayers, I began measuring big and small prayers with my running mileage. For example, a "small" request got ¼ mile of prayer coverage, a "medium" sized prayer equaled ½ mile, and a "larger" prayer received a full mile of talking to God. I divided my running route into ¼, ½, and full mile sections to lift up my prayer requests for that day.

My running/talking to God time began after high school when I realized that being an adult also meant I needed to own my spiritual quest. My "quarter-mile prayers" included educational exams, finding lost things, weather related events, and finances. "Half-mile prayers" were often about employment, pending decisions, courage, relationship beginnings, or healing after relationship break-ups. "Full mile prayers" often encompassed life and death situations, more serious health conditions, and grieving processes. On my prayer scale, those weighted issues needed more mileage. As I ran and talked to God about various people or situations I caught myself inserting solutions or thoughts into the situation. Soon I'd be mentally jogging all over the map of my own mind, worrying or calculating instead of praying for God's vantage point.

To redirect my haphazard thoughts, I repeated: "if 'x' is big enough to worry about, it's big enough to pray about. If 'x' is big enough to think about, it's big enough to talk to God about." My undisciplined thoughts created a non-productive trap. I learned that I'd gain more positive momentum if I turned those thoughts into prayer. God could do far more with my prayer press release than from my running on the proverbial hamster wheel.

Through more regular conversations with God, I discovered that most of my pleas stemmed from negative words or actions. Somebody said something hurtful. Someone acted without thinking. Another person reacted with harshness. Someone was overlooked or not cared for. Seeing another person hurting or grieving inspires me to be part of a construction team instead of a demolition crew. My core value focuses on building others up, not tearing them down; to encourage, not discourage.

I also learned to streamline my inner talk with a question: how does this person or situation invite a prayer? Prayer simplicity made life less complicated if I readily used that formula in my thinking. In first-grader terms? A smiley face sticker= Praise. A sad face sticker= Prayer. As I became more familiar with the Bible, I found Romans 8:28 NIV which teaches: "And we know that in all things God works for the good of those who love him, who have been called according to his purpose. That God causes *everything* to work together for the good of those who love God. A few things? Some things? No. *Everything*! Later in my Christian walk, I learned that God gets the last word, that He will be victorious despite any of my suffering. As a woman in my 20's at that time, I needed simplicity. I trimmed the spiritual complexity fat by challenging my thoughts to a duel: "praise or prayer?"

When a random thought crossed my mind: "Christina, is this thought praise worthy or a prayer opportunity?" When I'd get distracted, or mull something over and over (and sometimes over and over and over and over…), I began to train my mind to grab that restless thought and guide my thinking pattern by asking, "praise or prayer?" After I brought to light whatever I was pondering, I could better organize my thoughts and develop an intentional game plan that could move me forward. Mulling without action mentally chained me to a windowless cell as I prayed for open windows to new realms of insight.

One Sunday morning, I was paging through a New Believer's Bible while waiting for church service to begin. The author used the acronym THINK as a discerning tool for engaging in discussion:

T Is what I'm saying *true*?

H Are my words *helpful*?

I Will my input provide *insight*?

N Is what I'm saying *necessary*?

K Are my words *kind*?

That acronym made me sit a little straighter in the church seat that morning. It was time to spend my words like coins. I wanted to use each "coin" (word) wisely, to invest in long-term returns, to inspire rather than devalue. I had allowed my word spending to get out of hand and I needed a prayer meeting with my Financial Advisor about helping me put my money where my mouth was! It was time to tighten my word budget.

In disciplining my mouth to flex self-control muscle, I recognized how much excessive talking took place (including the person standing in my running shoes). The "think before speaking" adage rang loudly. When I intentionally filtered my words through a praise or prayer strainer, I quickly recognized how much monkey chatter I exchanged. I don't want to portray that this revelation gained me a halo or I walked with a holier-than-thou persona because I received a bit of monkey chatter enlightenment. The word budget did, however, heighten my awareness about how frequently I commented on something that didn't move toward positive discussion. I also came face-to-face with how often my idle chatter didn't contribute benefit or value to the conversation. Similar to a cream-filled donut, my nonchalant comments filled space, but didn't provide lasting nutritional sustenance.

I noticed the "verbal white noise" especially in group gatherings. Abundant, not necessarily edifying, comments unraveled and a string of opinions wrapped around the conversational fabric. I watched people interrupting each other, sometimes repeating the same idea because they weren't listening to one speaker. Decibels rose and people added their two cents at an inflation rate that could make Wall Street executives gasp. If everyone was talking, who was listening? I readily admit when I am passionate about certain topics I fall into similar whirlwind patterns of disrespectful conversation. My active listening becomes more active, less listening. I have two ears and one mouth for a reason: listen twice as much as I talk.

To open or close my mouth? That is the question. The decision invites a quick evaluation. Will my input uplift or weigh the conversation down? I'm still learning to filter more of my word count through God. Are my thoughts weighted with pain or heavy with praise?

THE MEMORY BANK

Repetitive running steps helped develop my memory, which led to greater recall of names, numbers, and facts. I still benefit from this acquired recall especially in learning and retaining people's names. During certain stages of formal education, I was required to memorize large blocks of information. Before I'd head out for a run, I reviewed notes for an upcoming test and create a running cadence that matched the exam material I needed to memorize. I remembered how to multiply algebraic equations to the cadence, "ours is not to reason why, just invert and multiply." When test time came, I recalled information by gently tapping my foot to the rhythm I remembered from my morning run. This wasn't a foolproof method because at times, in an effort to drum up stored information, my toe tapping sounded more like foot pounding. Sound off!

A side step...Running isn't the only time my memory is most engaged. The shower becomes my inferno for active thought circulation. I'm not sure if the process of massaging head with shampoo stimulates brain waves or the steady stream of water relaxes my mind to produce a flood of creativity. Is anyone aware of a correlation between shutting off a stream of shower head water and memory lapse? What sudden mental disconnect happens between powerful shower insights and reaching for a towel? Does that towel absorb fluid motion of thoughts? Do those inspirations get washed down the drain?

Why is it that in my mind's eye I can write nearly a chapter of material while showering and by the time I wrap the towel around my body, pull back the shower curtain and step onto the rug, my recall slips from one chapter to barely a single articulate sentence? I vote for all construction companies to require a waterproof dry erase boards and markers to install in every shower.

Back from throwing in the towel...

Memorization and recall added benefits to other areas of my life after school. I still have my Grandma's home phone number memorized though she's moved to a nursing home and her new number didn't transfer. I recall friends' childhood home addresses and certain family license plate numbers.

The owner of a business I used to work for required every employee to learn a customer's name every day. It was mandatory policy to greet regular customers by first name. When I frequent a business, I welcome employees calling me by name. I'm especially grateful when they reference my real name, not some random name.

Memorization is highly essential when running in a new area since it's inconvenient to carry a map or interrupt mileage to ask for directions. I've refrained from potential inconveniences (translate: scary neighborhoods) because I recalled bulletin boards or odd-looking trees along my running route. Landmark recall prevents unintentional mileage extensions, also known as getting lost.

I share a memorizing mishap when I drove to watch Tig race one weekend. We traveled repeatedly to this track and knew its final turnoff was at a specific large blue pole shed and house. We knew it as "the left turn at the large blue house." *The* left turn at *the* blue house, as if there were no other left turns and no other blue houses in that long stretch of country road.

Typically we ride to races as a family, but for whatever reason I drove separately from the truck, trailer, and race car crew. I allotted extra time in case I got to the track early to run a couple of miles before subjecting myself to several hours of bleacher bottom in the track stands. The drive seemed to take longer and the dashboard clock confirmed that I should have been at the track 20 minutes prior. I kept my focus toward the left turn at the blue house.

Speed read past a potentially long story of asking directions more than once, adding an hour of travel time, and sixty miles on the car, I recognized the blue house (which was now a right-hand turned for reasons you can speculate). The blue house had been painted cream with white shutters since we were at the racetrack. The story remains a family joke whenever we use landmarks as directional cues. Someone responds with an adaptation of: "Hopefully the owners haven't gotten bold enough to paint their buildings since we drove there last time."

Meanwhile, back from the now yellow house, formerly known as the left turn at the blue house…

The running/learning combo deemed helpful when I took a sign language course. Like any foreign language intense amounts of practice is required to fully communicate. I didn't have deaf friends in my community, but I signed up for the class out of admiration for interpreters communicating a silent art form language. I was curious how symbols and signs created a vernacular. In my limited contact with the deaf community, I sadly admit that I was one of the people who tried talking louder, flailing my arms, and contorting my mouth into acrobatic positions to attempt an effective exchange.

After each sign language class, I used my run time to discreetly practice the alphabet and word formations. When the symbol required a more pronounced move, I'd visualize that action and virtually practice the word symbol. It may be more animated to fully engage a sign language conversation with myself while running, but this creates an unpopular stigma for all humankind!

I am exceptionally grateful I was born with the gift of physical hearing. There are other non-physical sections of me that are still working through voluntary deafness. I wanted (and needed) to amplify the volume of my soul voice. Dr. Chris Stephens, Senior Pastor of Faith Promise Church in East Tennessee, wrote *A Plan of Your Life.* This book unlocked a treasure chest of knowledge that helped me hear God more clearly. Dr. Stephens maps out a path to include quiet time, fasting, reading positive enrichment books, budgeting a tithe, community outreach, witnessing to others, and scripture memorization. He also encourages a yearly growth plan to gauge personal spiritual temperature (that gauge is to be used as an evaluation for the person sitting in your chair). I recognized, in a guilt free way, I needed to turn up my thermostat.

At best, I was lukewarm in my walk with the Lord so I created a rookie spiritual growth plan. My first challenge was memorizing one scripture verse a week. Each Saturday, I chose an area where I needed solid spirit breakthrough. I'd find a bible verse that applied to a character trait where I needed fine tuning (or complete overhaul in areas such as patience and gentleness). I utilized my running miles to let biblical truths strengthen my core, an internal and external cross training between words and action. I viewed scriptural strength training as converting memorization into movement, like fat into muscle. Running provided external growth. Greeting people, memorizing, praying, and increased optimistic thinking opened arteries. This new valve of circuit training became an aerobic workout for the complete heart!

PASSING THE BATON

The following important events of my life timeline are for another writing venue or conversation. For brevity, sonic speed through college graduation, meeting my soon-to-be-husband at Coca-Cola where we worked, our wedding, son Todd, and a few more jobs, I propel through about a decade of running.

My spiritual cardio continued to increase and I wanted Tig, my husband, to experience similar supernatural growth. I wanted our shared lives to enjoy a deeper plane and raise our marriage to a more intimate level. Tig is someone who connects better in shorter, more frequent bursts. I sought prayer methods that would engage him quickly without extended duration.

We "tried on" several prayer options, similar to stepping into a dressing room to find jeans that fit that would be worn regularly. I set one-minute devotionals at the breakfast table so he could read while eating. I forwarded him short emails authored by various Christian writers. I placed inspirational sayings on top of his coffee mug before work. I hung short positive stories on the fridge. I sowed internal growth seeds with belief they would produce two-fold harvest, one as a marital crop and one as bounty for our son Todd.

Our family was already in the habit of before meal prayers. When Todd was in kindergarten, we taught: "Come Lord Jesus. Be our guest. Let these gifts to us be blessed." As he became more proficient with this simple prayer, he'd speed through it, sounding more like a nursery rhyme than an invitation for Jesus' presence at mealtime. Sometimes I wondered if he carried a stop watch to the meal table to time how fast he said the prayer. I wondered if those words impacted his heart.

One evening, after our meal prayer, I challenged Todd and Tig to share three specific things they were thankful from their day. Health, home, food, family, and cars are all crucial blessings, but I asked them to contribute less obvious blessings. I offered examples such as someone letting them in front of a line, or finding a quarter on the street (pennies, nickels and dimes counted too!) I suggested maybe there were all green lights in their travels, or a test got postponed. Perhaps they received an unexpected compliment or our dog Charlie's happy greeting when they walked in the door. This gratitude challenge helped set a positive tone at dinner.

We actively sought daily uplifts that resembled a scavenger hunt. Throughout the day, we collected experiences that caused grateful pause. Tig and I discovered this meal prayer addition invited deeper dinner conversation. We heard many of our friends talk about their mealtimes being chaotic or how they rarely shared exchanges beyond quick news clips. I wanted to use our family time for growing instead of groaning.

With three of us bringing three positive recognitions, we had nine discussion starters to choose during each dinner. Through those intentional ice breakers, we learned how each other felt about social justice topics such as homelessness and drug use. We taught work ethic through job-related stories and classroom interaction. We received a pulse on each other's priorities stemming from how often thanks was offered for areas of interest. We discovered what pieces of life got our special attention.

Our level of graciousness grew as a family unit. I certainly don't want to create a skewed family portrait that's had all imperfections touched up and air brushed. We shared "intense fellowship" as every family does. We experience (experience purposely left in present tense) moments of parenting boot camp. Sometimes parental battles are a bit like being drafted and sent onto the front line. The same battle is most likely felt within the child at times when they watch imperfect parents navigate through a maze of effectively training children.

When Todd complained about our rules or decisions, we'd offer a syrupy explanation about how we understood his difficulties in raising good parents. We sappily encouraged him to continue reading his parenting magazines and persevere while he watched his parental units slowly rise to his level of standards. We reminded him he was going to spend more of his life away from our parental Army tent so we needed to teach survival to our rising soldier. He didn't appreciate our candid approach to his grumbling. We reminded him that this parenting rodeo was our first go-round too. We all needed to learn to rope and ride. This technique was far more sentimental than when we were tempted to retort:

"We're all in this learning curve together and we agree with your objections and whining! Your Dad and I ask that you immediately bring us both a Midol and a beer!" I don't drink beer and Tig doesn't make a habit of taking Midol so even our snarky retaliation wasn't uplifting or true!

Tig and I needed to pool our resources. If we were swimming as a divided team, primarily during those pre-teen years, we would have drowned in the parenting dunk tank. We looked to our teenager's original Maker for guidance. When we first agreed to pray as a couple about each aspect of Todd's life, it was awkward. Outside of our meal prayers, we didn't have experience talking to God in front of each other. We were desperate for family peace though so we practiced through a lot of simplistic communication, learned willingness and increased transparency with each other. We slowly developed a flow in talking with God.

We experimented with prayer methods including worship songs, Bible studies, parenting devotionals, and journaling so we could later witness how God answered our pleas. Through trial and error, we remained consistent. One of the approaches we created together was the "tennis match prayer." We still use it whenever we have a lot of praise and prayer, but not a lot of time to go into depth. It's a style of quickly touching base with each other and letting God know what's on our hearts.

The tennis match prayer begins simply by saying, "let's stop for a minute-long tennis match." One of us starts with a prayer or praise that dominates our minds. The tennis match begins with Tig saying something like: "I pray for Todd to be delivered from smoking." I follow up Tig's initial "serve" with something such as: "I ask for guidance in our discussion about curfew tonight." Tig returns the prayer ball with: "I'm thankful for holding my tongue when I was tempted to yell." We continued lobbing each other's serves until we exhaust every area that needs to be uncovered or recovered at the time. It has become a spiritual cardio workout that strengthened us individually as prayer warriors *and* as a couple fighting for the same purpose: to wholesomely raise our son. The volley for serve starts and ends with a score of love-love.

EXPANDING OUR HORIZONS

There's something intimate about sharing prayers with another person. It's opening up a room in your heart that is initially as comfortable as investigating a crawl space. What virtual spiders will we find in those crevices? Will there be treasure among the folds of my spouse's inner being? Will there be disappointing mold and debris that needs to be cleared? It's vulnerable enough to divulge certain *thoughts* with each other, but expressing heartfelt prayers was an abnormally raw initiative for Tig and me.

We did our best to live our marital vows to include sickness and health; for richer or for poorer; for better or for worse. We hung onto our marriage even when we questioned if worse was misspelled in our marriage vows (Did our 'wors' end with a *t* or an e?). The more regularly we used our tennis match prayer, the more confident we grow in praying in front of each other. We realized our need and want to expand prayer coverage beyond ourselves and family.

With another launch of boldness, we signed up for our church prayer ministry team. We saw the church's request for prayer warriors but hid behind reasons (aka excuses) that we weren't equipped to serve in a ministry as critical as standing in the gap for others. We found out God thought differently.

Over the next few weeks, my desire to be a part of the prayer team increased. I invited Tig to join me for the outreach training as a ministry we could explore together. When it comes to decision making, Tig is a silent observer who assesses all elements of a situation before making a commitment. He prefers to digest information, ponder it, and then decide. It's rare for him to make an on-the-spot declaration. He surprised me when he agreed to sign up for the next prayer team training.

Each prayer team member signs up to pray in the church prayer room for one-hour time slots. During that hour, people are invited to read spiritual growth books, listen to worship music, pray from the requests in the church prayer journal, or reflect on whatever God places on someone's heart. Tig and I found solitude in the prayer room hour as we kneeled or sat in God's presence. We also discovered our eyelids growing heavy in that peaceful prayer room, sometimes nodding off and then groggily trying to recapture our focus. We wanted to be warriors who battled with dynamite enthusiasm, not two lukewarm noodles sitting idly on a cooled stove.

Tig and I decided to blend our nighttime walk with spiritual movement. During our weekly evening prayer time we walked around the church exterior using our tennis match prayer for the first half hour. After our prayer walk, we completed the second half of the hour with quiet meditation and reading in the prayer room. We discovered the late evening prayer watch provided unexpected transparency. For whatever reason, Tig and I were less guarded to speak openly to God as we walked under the dark sky. We also didn't have the distraction of people engaging in church activities that typically happened earlier in the evening.

I was amazed at what God put on our hearts during that half-hour. I was equally excited to unashamedly share specific prayers. Previously, vulnerability would have been too raw to verbally express in front of each other. We talked to God about each pastor, church leadership, small groups, church finances, wisdom for designing programs, pastors' families, church member requests, and everything in between. While walking the exterior, Tig and I asked God for a hedge of protection around our church to keep predators out. Inside, during the second half-hour, we spiritually secured the church interior, asking for strengthened foundation among the church body.

At the risk of using a well-worn cliché, we began understanding "the couple who prays together, stays together." Through this prayer walk experience with Tig, I gradually let go of personal insecurity. Prior to our prayer ministry experience, I feared losing his unconditional love if he found out what scuffles raged in my mind. Tig is the least judgmental person I've ever met. I trust him. I respect him, yet I secretly feared if he saw more of my weaknesses, he'd hightail from my life.

Through this prayer platform, I became secure enough to share some of my journal entries. I've asked for his wisdom after reading my written internal dialogue without feeling like I just swallowed an entire pineapple. For the record, I have not consumed an unpeeled pineapple, but this was the first visual that popped in my head as I pictured my initial comfort level in divulging parts of my journal to Tig. We now return you to your regularly scheduled program…

ROLL WITH THE CHANGES

I find it intriguing to watch life trends, changes, and reminisce the past while anticipating the future. I use my past journal entries to contemplate a collection of thankfulness, prayers, creative ideas, and lessons. I also watch for documented 'opportunities for growth' as I see how God moved and carried me through a pitfall. Too often, in the midst of a valley, I focus on the slippery mud, instead of reflecting on the light above. My only guideline in journaling is that the first entry is something I'm happy or grateful. Even on days when I'm most distracted or upset, I sit with that open journal waiting until some specific positive aspect of my life comes to mind to write. Looking back on some of the entries, I can see the mornings I struggle to build joy into that day's foundation. A couple entries stand out: "I am thankful the squawking crows became my back-up alarm when my alarm clock didn't go off" and "Thank God for carpet instead of hardwood floors in January."

Sometimes in weary desperation, I flip through previous journal entries to read what challenges I've faced or overcome. In seeing past victories in writing, I'm guarded against getting stuck in a funk. The highlights become a palpable caffeine boost for my soul. Paging through my prayer journal is like looking through a photo album of my life's written snapshots. I see a prayer request that has been resolved then write in the margin a brief caption about how the prayer was answered.

I also use my prayer journal to remember great ideas, or at least ideas I think are great. An imaginative thought will come to me and I'll write the inspiration under the praise section, "thank you for the idea to…" The journal becomes a one-source hub to reference brainstorms without hunting through scraps of napkins, envelope backs and whatever else I grabbed at the time to write I-need-to-remember-this thought. The process helps compartmentalize my thoughts so I record it in a system that validates current brain wave, but understands the thought is categorized as save-for-later.

Tangent alert. During the tedious process of writing this book, re-reading, editing, re-reading, rewriting, I've waffled in the decision to share this New Year's party for two. Our friends know about the way Tig and I celebrate New Year's and we've gotten reactions spanning from: "aw, isn't that sweet," to "maybe other people would like try that idea," to "really, that sounds like an episode directly out of a Leave it To Beaver script!" Tig is on board with me sharing our tradition so carrying on…

A form of journaling birthed a New Year's Eve tradition that Tig and I still honor. In the 1990's, I bought a large block calendar to jot down highlights from each day of that year. At year end, I asked Tig if he wanted to talk about those events I had written on the calendar. We spent that New Year's Eve recapping memories and adding stories about what stood out in our mind.

Since then, on New Year's Eve, Tig and I sit in our living room with a snack buffet, bottle of wine, and current year calendar to review the notes I've kept on each day. There are a few features from last year's calendar that made it to the Eder large block datebook: Oreo brownies to Tig's office; new entry way light; Todd home from Cheyenne; Amy visit admissions rep; Eunice move furniture. For most people, these vague bullet points merely raise eyebrows. To Tig and I, these will spark many conversations. The comments and stories become even more animated after we start a second glass of wine!

What is most fun about this New Year's tradition is to swap feedback with each other *after* the encounters. A situation that deemed worthwhile enough to write may prove itself extraordinary or extremely unimportant by New Year's Eve. The calendar review is our historical tapestry woven from few words. The back side of our family tapestry was written on the calendar during each string of life being spun. By year end, as the tapestry of events expanded, Tig and I look beyond individual strings and see a fuller picture. Those individual strings were knit to color our history with new shades and textures. My perspective is one snapshot while Tig holds a different perception of the same experience. Some memories lead to recall and fresh discussion. A few dates cause us to breathe a sigh of relief as ones we'd rather forget. From either perspective, the calendar review becomes our yearly photo album as we verbally reminisce the past 365 days of our lives. We typically keep the calendar for a few months after

New Year's Eve and then it goes into our spring paper declutter, toss, and recycle bin.

BUILDING BLOCKS

A friend gave me a soft leather journal with a satin ribbon and golden rimmed pages. The cover was etched with Jeremiah 29:11 ("I know the plans I have for you declares the Lord). This gift was too elaborate to use as one of my everyday diaries and I wanted to fill it with timeless written treasures to use as a valuable resource. Shortly after she gave me that gift, I was introduced to devotionals and various Christian sermons. These abundant selections of wisdom fed me spiritual nutrition that I wanted to thoroughly digest. In that new learning log, I wrote inspirational quotes, interpretations of scripture that captured my attention, captivating sermon notes, and devotionals filled with meat and potatoes. Instead of piling these gems into a shoebox of hodge podge to read 'one day', I immediately wrote these building blocks into my learning log. I still reference material from that first collection of my learning journal.

I'd love to copy that handwritten learning log and invite each reader to glean whatever literary tidbits he or she needs. Instead of adding about 200 pages of text, I carefully perused that journal for entries that I consider the "best of the best" wisdom. I hope these will refresh and inspire you. When an author was listed from a source, I credited their name here. Named or unnamed, I ask God to bless the author in a special way out of gratitude for their writing. Their words continue providing strength for my Christian walk (or case being, my Christian run).

☐ Matthew 7:7(NIV): "Ask and it will be given you." One of the reasons we don't see miracles in our lives is because we don't ask. Before you pay for it, pray for it. Give God a chance to give it to you before you go out and charge it. Let God take charge!

☐ Luke 6:38(NIV): "Give, and it will be given to you. A good measure, pressed down, shaken together and running over, will be poured into your lap. For with the measure you use, it will be measured to you." Many of us act like spiritual orphans. We forget that we have a heavenly Father who already knows what we need. Birds don't run around saying, "I'd better build a bigger nest for retirement." I have yet to see a stressed-out bird. Worry is a form of atheism because it indicates that life depends on yourself.

☐ From Dr. Chris Stephens' 8-28-10 sermon about procrastination: The Bible gives us 5 reasons for delay:

1. Indecision: a double-minded man is unstable in all he does (i.e. ordering in a restaurant, choosing a college, buying a vehicle.)

2. Perfectionism: if you wait for the perfect conditions, you'll never get anything done. We don't have enough time or money for things to be perfect before you make a move.

3. Fear: postponing a dentist appointment, meeting with a marriage counselor, sharing faith, fear that you don't deserve good, fear of criticism, fear of too much responsibility. Ask yourself, "What am I afraid of?"

4. Anger: procrastination is passive resistance or possibly getting back at people we don't like. Challenge question: Is one of the people you don't

like yourself? Learn to healthily love yourself and watch yourself move!

5. Laziness: Prov. 13:4 teaches that lazy people want much but get little while the diligent are prospering. Ask God to help you overcome any laziness so you can propel forward.

☐God will take care of yesterday's failures, today's frustrations, and tomorrow's fears.

☐When people aren't in your heart, they end up on your nerves.

☐Hear the heart, listen to the hurt. If you care, you'll be aware.

☐A sharp tongue is the quickest way to cut a throat. Stop, look, listen!

Stop: angry words always seem to come easily.

Look: See the situation from God's point of view. It is His glory to overlook an offense.

Listen: Any angry person is just a hurting person. When you listen to the frustration, it's easier to respond instead of react angrily.

☐God's love turns crucifixions into resurrections.

☐HOPE: An acronym for Holding On, Praying Expectedly.

☐Pastor Rick Warren: "Until you know what you are willing to die for, you are not ready to live."

☐Jesus told the apostles to be fishers of men. The enemy is also fishing for men. The difference between Jesus and the enemy is in their fishing styles: Jesus uses a soft but extremely sturdy net to scoop. The enemy uses a spear hook to capture and scar.

☐Prov. 10:27: Reverence for God adds hours to each day. When you're overloaded by activity, you are in survival mode. You only think of yourself, which limits your usefulness in your ministry. When you have no downtime and God taps you on the shoulder saying, "I'd like you to do this for me," your first reaction may likely be, "another thing to do? Sorry God, I'd love to help you, but I'm just too busy." We end up resenting great opportunities that God brings to our lives. When we build a buffer around our own schedule, we become available for God to use us.

☐Lasting change doesn't start with you, it starts with God. Change begins when we say, "Yes, Lord, I'm taking you at your Word." God isn't asking you to *make* a promise you can't keep. He is asking you to *receive* a promise only *He* can keep.

☐The world has four primary standards used to evaluate (aka judge) a person:

1. Appearance: beauty = value
2. Affluence: owning a lot = worth a lot
3. Achievement: trophies, awards, certificates
4. Approval: how many people like me? (pre-Facebook times meant approval was something more than a simple click of a button to indicate a "like"). Beauty fades with age, possessions wear out, someone else's success will exceed your success, and not everyone will like you. Humans tend to base self-esteem on what the most important person their life thinks of them. Make Jesus the most important person in your life because He will always tell you the truth. See yourself the way God sees you!

☐ When you are going through any problem or pain, play it down and pray it up. Minimize the pain, maximize the profit.

☐ When Satan gives you thoughts, they are called temptations. When God gives you thoughts, they are called inspirations.

☐ G.K. Chesterton: "When belief in God becomes difficult, the tendency is to turn away from Him. But turn to what? The skeptic? To the one who has been disappointed in his faith?"

☐ When God wants to make a mushroom, He takes six hours. When God wants to make an oak tree, He takes 60 years. Solid foundational changes are not going to happen overnight.

☐ A belief is something you will argue about. A conviction is something you will die for. Your convictions determine your conduct. Irony is when people have strong convictions about weak things (football and fashion) while they hold weak convictions about major things (right and wrong).

☐ Pastor Rick Warren: "God sends the rain when He needs to soften people's hearts. Anytime you see someone going through a storm, you can know God is softening a heart."

☐ Jesus was comfortable grabbing a towel instead of grabbing the spotlight.

☐ 3 John 1:5 (MSG): "When you extend hospitality to Christian brothers and sisters, even when they are strangers, you make the faith visible." Any time we give money to God, it draws us closer to God. Any time we invest in another person (writing a note of encouragement, taking someone to lunch, listening to the heart of another person, sending a card) we are investing in God's mutual fund.

☐ Pastor Bayless Conley in Answers for Each Day online devotional. GO: Gospel to Others. Mark 16:15 (NIV): "Go into all the world and preach the gospel to every creature, making you fishers of men." Do you GO to pristine lakes where you can catch fish or set up an incredible campsite? In order to get fish, you have to go to the water. No one catches fish while sitting at camp. A lot of Christians just hang around camp. They form fishing clubs and talk about how important it is to fish, but they don't fish. You can talk about what lures you'll use, how you'll cook them fish after you catch them, but if you never thrown a line in the water, you'll never catch a fish. GO fish!

☐ Missionary Mehdi Dibaj: The more I visit Him up there, the more I experience His help down here. People say I was a Muslim from my birth. God says I am a Christian from the beginning."

☐ Martin Luther King: "One plus God equals a majority. Ordinary you, extraordinary God. When you see God in His greatness, even giants look as small as grasshoppers. It's good to acknowledge your problems, but it is wrong and dangerous to focus all your attention on them."

☐ Heaven is too real. Hell is too hot. Eternity is too long. People are too lost. Life is too short for us not to be actively engaged in reaching people. The only things we take to heaven are the precious souls we reach for Christ.

☐ The first step in discovering and understanding life's mission is to ask: "What grieves my heart?"

Paul was grieved about the city of Athens given over to idols; Job's heart was grieved for the poor; David's heart was grieved as Goliath taunted the Israelites. Generally the things that grieve you in your spirit are the very things that God has gifted you to change for the better.

☐ By nature, we want to escape suffering and avoid pain. An old proverb says, "If you want life, expect pain." Hardships are not meant to *defeat* us, they are meant to *develop* us."

☐ Phillip Brooks: "I do not pray for a lighter load. I pray for a stronger back."

☐ Corrie ten Boom: "When I try, I fail. When I trust, He succeeds."

Each entry in my learning journal became a building block for my growth. Stacking these building blocks was like swallowing a vitamin to nourish spiritual muscle while I ran. This visual gives new meaning to soul food. I continue adding inspirational nuggets to learning journals and steep my mind in thought development (random as those thoughts can sometimes be)!

FRUIT OF THE SPIRIT

This book stemmed from running miles and lessons logged during a 30 year harvest of journaling. Maybe if I build a stronger core, I'll be less likely to be a bad apple. Enough fruity comments...time to get down to business.

During my sophomore year of college, an economics' professor assigned the class to each list our top 100 lifetime dreams and goals. Initially, this project seemed fun and fairly simple. At 20 years old, my life's perception was synonymous with dreams and goals. Some days I worried that 100 years (give or take) wouldn't be enough time to experience and achieve all I wanted. I quickly scribbled down 12 or 13 aspirations, took a few minutes to write down 6 or 7 more, and then wham! I hit a mental guard rail head-on. Suddenly my sense of logic fell into the economic equation. I started second guessing finances, logistics, education, schedules, and factors I couldn't control to make these dreams possible. The whiplash of practicality stopped me dead in my goal-setting tracks.

I bypassed the detour of practical thinking long enough to complete the Top 100 homework list and learn how my aspirations can affect the overall economy. The professor pointed out how the use of time and money contributed (negatively and positively) to the nation. The assignment was utilized to stretch our thinking from individualized relativity to a broader world economic relationship. That economics assignment became a conceptualized learning seed that later birthed dreams and goal workshops.

After completing that college class project, I wanted to hear what life wishes stirred the spirit in other people. Economics is important, but I yearned to learn what wealth came from someone else's exchange rate of dreams. To test the market, I asked friends to a Dream and Goal theme party one weekend. I made snacks and challenged each friend to list their lifetime aspirations. I passed out fun printed paper numbered from 1-100 and presented the goals idea as my professor had, but without the economic implication. One friend said she wanted to see her favorite band in concert. Her idea sparked another someone else's fire about a place she wanted to visit. Soon a myriad of other travel destinations entered the goal mix. Someone piped in about a class he wished to take, leading other dreamers to discuss educational pursuits.

Fresh lively conversation lit that evening as we invested a few hours in simply dreaming together. We talked about life beyond our usual surface level of social interaction. We got to discover new layers of each other's heart. Someone suggested ongoing dream parties so we could hold each other accountable, network ideas, and achieve some of our dreams together. They wanted to support and experience each other's ventures and goal chasing partnerships were created. The energy flow was contagious!

During my run the next morning, I drafted an invitation to other groups who may be interested in a dream workshop. I wanted to present the class as a playground for soul recreation. I wanted others to capture the free spirit my friends and I encountered the night before. I couldn't run fast enough that morning because I wanted to get home and write all rapidly firing thoughts to share with my newly created dream partners.

Fast forward past several weeks of polling people to test the dream party and goal setting workshop. After a few word-of-mouth invitations and posted fliers, I was delighted when a women's group asked me to share this dream and goal workshop. During that seminar, a common thread that tethered people from launching out of their comfort zone was the four letter word…fear. The workshop participants expressed reasonable hesitations for not pursuing their dreams: What about funds? What if someone laughs at my idea? Is it normal not to have a big dream? What if I fail? What if I succeed? How will I find the time? Will I appear selfish if I work on my own goals before someone else's needs or wants?

Instead of addressing the participant's concerns with a non-reassuring (but truthful) canned reply: "but you'll never know unless you try," I left that workshop seeking deeper wisdom. I wanted to find an answer when people asked me: "How do you find the courage and determination to keep pursuing your dreams when you're scared and/or have other priorities? I get discouraged (i.e. an unaccounted for block of time that doesn't coincide with a paycheck to cover the goal's expenditure or vice-versa). Sometimes I wonder if I'll ever achieve dreams that have remained on my original goal list (i.e. take an African jungle safari, travel to Switzerland).

I find many, if not most, solutions through music. This universal language covers some need on every layer of my emotional spectrum. This melodic answer may not cut a record for "Most Influential Solutions", but music tuned me into an educational tool. I use songs to create natural breaks between instructional blocks during dream and goal seminars.

One set of lyrics may gift someone with a much needed cry. Another song may uplift or soothe someone's heart. I encourage workshop participants to use music to match their spirit's needs. I want individuals to find their answers through musical guidance and tapping into personal wisdom as they develop persistent courage and discernment toward their life's purpose/calling/destiny/dreams.

Depending on the age and audience, I select songs to encourage an inspirational face-off with condescending self-talk. The following playlists are "My Top 10 Fear-Fighting Songs." One list invokes my evolving tenacity. The other list is played on gritty days when I need to have the sand kicked out of my britches.

List One

Don't Stop Believing by Journey

Voice of Truth by Casting Crowns

Brave by Nichole Nordmann

Standing Outside the Fire by Garth Brooks

I'm Moving On by Rascal Flatts

Do It Anyway by Martina McBride

I Will Survive by Gloria Gaynor

Broken Wing by Martina McBride

The River by Garth Brooks

It's My Life by Bon Jovi

List Two

In Constant Sorrow by the Soggy Bottom Boys

Kiss This by Aaron Tippin

Insensitive by Jann Arden

Hakuna Matata by Timone and Pumba on the Lion King (I love singing both Timone and Pumba's parts in their different character voices!)

Courtesy of the Red, White, and Blue by Toby Keith

Thunder Road by Bruce Springsteen

Young Turks by Rod Stewart

Heads Carolina, Tails California by Jo Dee Messina

One Hot Mama by Trace Adkins

All Summer Long by Kid Rock

During our seminars, I challenge participants to temporarily suspend reality while they create their Top 100 Lifetime Dreams and Goals List. When strict practicality enters a dream picture, pure delicious joy of mental recreation diminishes.

Daydreaming can be a virtual vacation, taking our minds to new places and challenging ourselves with fresh perspective.

Logic and discernment are crucial, but for maximum creativity to surface, sometimes practicality stifles free-flow dreaming processes. During the seminar when I promote a broader vision for life, participants switch from workshop to playground mode. It's the segment of class where time, money, location, child care, age, education, and other constraints are suspended while we indulge our minds in a mini vacation. We take recess to momentarily release our best daydreaming energy. I share this section of my dreams workshop with eagerness that you'll take the lid off your mental captivity jar and release inspiration.

First, grab a journal or printed paper that speaks life to you. Bright colors, dog photos, funny quotes, symbols, whatever makes you smile when you see it. Choose a pen that you use to note only your dreams. Please use a pen that glides across the paper, not the ones that skip ink or bleed dye globs onto your paper and fingers (those hit-or-miss pens may have inspired part of this book's title). In a pinch, a black sharpie or perhaps a jumbo green crayon that you fish from the kitchen junk drawer works, but it's more appealing to dream when you have that special writing utensil. Next, give in to the luxury of distancing yourself from other people or potential distractions. Wal-Mart on a Saturday afternoon or Chuck E Cheese mid-birthday party are typically not first-choice options for lofty hopes beyond survival.

Sometimes it's helpful to visualize yourself at the top of a tall tree and invite your spirit to capture your dream perception from several feet above the rest of the world. If you're afraid of heights, a sandy beach at sunset or a garden gazebo at sunrise may be more appealing to dream from a new perspective. Whatever you need to engage in this mini retreat, I encourage you to draw upon those resources.

Here we go!

- Write the first 10 things that come to your mind that you most want to experience during your lifetime (those dreams and goals you talk about most often but this time you're writing them down)
- List 5 places anywhere in the world you'd like to see
- List 3 people you'd love to meet (or meet again)
- List 3 jobs you'd enjoy trying, or 3 jobs you'd like to shadow
- List 5 books you want to read
- List 4 skills you'd like to learn
- List 3 hobbies you'd like to try
- List 2 restaurants you'd like to visit

After this initial visit to your soul, you'll have 35 ideas to explore. I encourage each person to keep this list readily available and as new dreams surface, write those gems on this canvas of lifetime aspirations. Train your eyes to be like a camera to capture those moments when you say, "I'd like to try that" or "I'd love to see that." Before that snapshot disappears behind the screen of practicality filter, I urge you to immediately record that dream.

The dream list is started…now what? In addition to fear, the next question during seminars is, "Now what do I do with this?"

I urge people to get an accountability person, a trusted someone. I believe the ideal dream supporter is non-judgmental; encourages without pressuring; actively listens; someone who will network a dream to fruition; maybe even a person willing to join the dreamer on a quest. I've had the honor of traveling with girlfriends on their adventures simply by saying yes to an excursion they wanted to experience with someone else.

After dream and goal seminars, I find it nearly impossible not to jump up and down as participants recap their contagious passion for a rekindled pursuit. It's nearly impossible not to leap onto their enthusiastic energy train to ride toward their cause, creation, or voyage.   I love watching people's potential explode.

On the home front, my husband and I have kept a 100 Lifetime Dreams and Goals list since 1996. We update and redefine our dreams, sometimes adding a few comments about the revision. When we achieve a goal, we highlight the dream, put a date next to it, and add notes about the experience. As previously mentioned, we celebrate New Year's Eve by reviewing our past year's calendar and our dream lists. We star three dreams to work toward each year. We choose one relatively-easy-to-accomplish dream, one moderate goal, and one aspiration that require additional resources needed. An "easy dream" means simply being more intentional in scheduling or putting the money aside for the event or activity. For example, an easy dream could be reading a specific book or eating at a new restaurant. One moderate goal includes hiking a trail that requires more than a few hours or increased physical training. A larger, more in-depth aspiration consists of a trip to Ireland or taking an Alaskan cruise.

A side note: I categorized learning to knit on my easy-to-moderate stretch level. I've tried knitting four different times at four phases of my life. With each of those four stages, with four different instruction methods, I've discovered all four times that knitting needles are best used as tomato stakes or self-defense weapons. It was "knot" a dream but more like an intensely frustrating nightmare. Thus, I learned something new.

When I pass from this earth, I requested to have my 100, now 107, Lifetime Dreams and Goals list displayed at my celebration of life. I want my earthly journey to represent wise use of air, space, and energy. I'm inspired by a "well- seasoned" friend's response: "Patricia, are you ever going to slow down?" She fires back her answer with spunk: "Oh *honey*, when I get to heaven, I want to be completely empty of all God put into me. I'm gonna slide into those Pearly Gates and holler, "Hallelujah Lord, I used all Your time, money, energy, talent, all of everything You gave me. I'm tired, but I made it and whew! You talk about a tremendous ride! Let me in! " Like Patricia, I want to actively live, not passively exist.

A MOVING BILLBOARD

If I want to shift Patricia's inspiration to life transformation, I inventory areas I've passively existed. I prefer solo activities and require copious amounts of quiet time. I appreciate people, like being invited to outings, and once I get to the event, it's typically enjoyable. My chasm between living and existing lies in lack of patience for idle talk. I am irritated by muddling through surface layer conversations. Instead of accepting these first few minutes of polite but awkward dialogue, I avoid many social situations. My boxed-in limitations squelch the 'ride the exhilarating waves of life' that Patsy describes.

Instead of a default, "That's just the way I am," I began looking at what transpired during start-up conversations. After the weather, job, kids, general busy chatter, a hover craft of silent space landed. In error, I wanted every conversation to include the depth that came from teaching dream and goal seminars or life coaching. Realizing that expectation was unrealistic and in some cases, out of place, I looked for one line quotes or odd tidbits to create a more vibrant opening line. If icebreaker chats were going to be tedious, I wanted to work through my discomfort by using an interesting quip that was appropriately unusual.

I have a bulletin board in our home office to post odd facts such as, "Intelligent people have more zinc and copper in their hair." I use these musings and motivational quotes as conversational drivers in social gatherings, hopefully placing weather and traffic chatter in the back seat. Most of the time, this quip and quote approach has been well received.

Using discretion based on audience and gathering venue, these are some of my bulletin board favorites:

*What do bullet proof vests, fire escapes, windshield wipers, and laser printers all have in common? All were invented by women.

*The first couple to be shown in bed together on prime time television was Fred and Wilma Flintstone. (An author side note: this may not be appropriate at Pastor Appreciation dinners).

*The state with the highest percentage of people who walk to work is Alaska.

*It takes 3000 cows to supply the NFL with enough leather for a year's supply of footballs.

*Snails can sleep for three years without eating (not to be talked about at a clinic when someone is fasting before blood work)

*Months that begin on a Sunday will always have a Friday the 13th.

*There are 293 ways to make change for $1.

*A cat has 32 muscles in each ear.

*No word in the English language rhymes with month, orange, silver, or purple.

*"Stewardesses" is the longest word typed with only the left hand and "lollipop" with your right hand.

Along with interesting facts that people somehow discover, I appreciate intriguing quotes to combat small talk. These fascinating one or two liners become word art for my mind during my running, somewhat like verbal energy bars.

"Laughter is a tranquilizer with no side effects." – Arnold Glasgow

"Failure doesn't mean you are a failure…it just means you haven't succeeded yet." –Robert Schuller

"My obligation is to do the right thing. The rest is in God's hands." Martin Luther King, Jr.

"Problems are only opportunities in work clothes." –Henry Kaiser

"Millions saw the apple fall, but Newton was the one who asked why." –Bernard Baruch

"I will not permit any man to narrow and degrade my soul by making me hate him." –Booker T. Washington

"Don't let your learning lead to knowledge, let your learning lead to action." –Jim Rohn

"A prayer not answered is simply a prayer not prayed." –Anonymous

"The bigger a man's head, the worse is his headache." –Persian Proverb

"Waste your money and you're only out of money. Waste your time and you've lost a part of your life." –Michael Lebouef

"Standing in the middle of the road is very dangerous; you get knocked down by the traffic on both sides." –Margaret Thatcher

These conversation stimulators come in handy on Saturday night date nights when Tig and I are glad to be together, but too tired to articulate meaty conversation. These also serve as neutral topics when we've faced a day that could result in a stream of negative spewing.

Life's Too Short for Dull Razors, Cheap Pens, and Worn Out Underwear | Christina Eder

LIFE IN THE FAST LANE

I was introduced to fasting and the impact of negative talk nearly simultaneously. I had a habit of putting nutritious and balanced foods *into* my mouth (balance includes dark chocolate Hershey kisses). I wish I could say the same for what came *out* of my mouth at times when I should use both running shoes for my lips instead of my feet.

Even as a committed runner, I never fully understood the discipline to fast. I consider myself regimented because I run in undesirable weather conditions. I discipline myself to snack on celery and peanut butter more often than brownies or fried onion rings. If I stay up past my 9:00 bedtime, I avoid the temptation to skip the next morning's run. Despite these practices, I wasn't buying the concept of food abstinence. Our pastor preached about the value of fasting; I read about Jesus fasting in the desert; I heard testimonies about people receiving major breakthroughs from fasting.

In an effort to be more open minded about disciplining my flesh, I gave the fasting process a try. Looking back, I'm humbled that I thought fasting was simply going through a day without eating. Translate: starve for 1440 minutes, count the hours until breakfast the next day, anticipate spiritual movement, and hope the revelation is too obvious to miss. I used this misguided perception to abstain from food on Fridays. Friday was my muscle recovery day and without running, I thought this day made the most sense to pray and fast.

I particularly remember the first Friday I embarked the fasting journey because more coworkers brought more food that day. I chalked up this out-of-the-ordinary recipe sharing as possibly some enemy sabotage against my first fasting experience. At that point in my Christian walk, I had learned a few concepts about spiritual warfare. I confess I was feeling a little full of my self-control as I watched treats being carried to the break room. I smugly thought that the influx of decadent food was Satan's trap to set me up to fail this fasting initiation.

All morning, I watched people parading through the office with various desserts, cheese and cracker platters, fruit trays. I internally scoffed about being stronger than mere food temptations. Besides, my office was far enough from the break room that I couldn't smell the aromas. Disregard my previous claims about high tolerance for goal straying. I ventured into that break room just to prove I could withstand temptations. The first walk past the food counter was simple because it was early morning when desserts looked too sweet for my taste buds. Temptation factor: low.

A couple hours later I tested my willpower again. This time, strolling past the food displays was appealing but not overly tempting. By lunch time, my stomach, which was used to eating every 3-1/2 hours, had a virtual question mark that started rumbling around. I couldn't swear to it, but I think I heard my stomach holler, "Ahem! Did you forget? It's been four hours since I got fuel. According to your eating pattern, you're supposed to be refueling me right now!"

Knowing I didn't need to unnecessarily tease myself, I retreated to my office. I purposely tackled a project requiring intense focus to side track my slight hunger pangs. I wasn't feeling spiritual. I found myself battling harder to fight my body's low fuel light. Mid-afternoon rolled around and my persistent stomach knocked on its wall questioning: "Hello? Are we still friends? We have a contract here. Remember? I grumble, you feed me. At least throw me a bone!" I was fatigued but answered my stomach's grumbling with large gulps of water.

I reminded myself this discomfort was part of the fasting experience. I wasn't giving in to hunger pangs that hindered these benefits I heard so much about. People who fasted regularly said they felt cleansed and a sense of purification, increased clarity around ponderous questions, and revelation about God's direction for their lives. I sought positive testimony too!

I pressed on toward evening and cooked my husband's dinner quickly so kitchen time was as limited as possible. In addition to fatigue and more persistent stomach growls, I was getting lightheaded. I convinced myself this wobbly sensation was for "the greater good." Although I had no definition of what the greater good really meant, I was determined to become a fasting warrior. As the night wore on, I grew irritable, hungrier, and unfocused. Instead of fighting through these annoyances, I huffed off to bed shortly after 8:00.

Saturday morning, I woke up minimally impressed and maximally famished from the fasting hangover. Instead of my typical early morning run, I ate a lumberjack sized breakfast and postponed my run so my body could adjust its blood flow, sugar and energy levels. I was so worn down from living only on water and a multi-vitamin that during my morning journaling, I was hard pressed to find any anticipated bells and whistles from the fasting experience. Instead, I was disappointed by the physical drag colliding with emotional letdown. Since it was my first fasting rodeo, I pulled myself up by the boot straps and prepared to ride more solidly into the next Friday.

The following Thursday night I prepared for the Friday fast by creating positive mental pictures. I visualized myself strong, smiling through weaknesses, and solidly engaging in this week's fast. I made a list of questions I sought answers and asked God to give me people and causes to pray about instead of my focus on missing meals. Mind over matter. I would not be a slave to food.

Sadly, by midday Friday, I was physically feeling worse than I had the previous Friday. By noon, I was dizzy and ready to chew someone's head off for lunch. As Friday dragged on, I feared I wasn't as disciplined as I originally thought. I questioned if my determination was over-confident. I worried my flesh was weaker than I perceived. I doubted my internal strength. Was this feebleness selfish? Were other people's fasting testimonies false? Did they sugar coat their experience or downplay symptoms of "crucifying their flesh?"

I would not let 24 hours without food get in the way of personal growth. I hit the following Friday with a vengeance. My updated game plan was to utilize every Friday for a specific outreach. Whenever a physical sign would rear its head, I'd use that indicator as a reminder to pray for the "cause of the week." For example, one week I prayed for the physically hungry. Throughout that day whenever I experienced a bodily pang, I filled that gap with opportunity to pray for those who endured more than 24 hours without food.

Another week, I prayed for single moms and orphans. Some weeks, I dedicated the Friday fast to military; emergency workers; church pastors; or teachers. This list may sound heroic, but I was grumpy, weak, ill, and fuzzy headed. Sometimes on Fridays, I counted hours until bedtime to gain relief from hunger pains. I resented Saturday mornings because prior to fasting, I ran extended mileage routes because Saturday mornings were when I was less scheduled. I was now too exhausted from Friday to withstand those longer runs. Thursdays, I started doubling standard food portions in an effort to stave off, or at least lessen, Friday's anticipated pain. Was this intense irritability negating any positive impact that fasting was supposed to generate? When I woke one Thursday morning with immediate dread of what I faced the following day, I knew something needed to change.

My motive and pure intentions were meant for strengthening, but I was failing miserably in my method to grow positive impact. In the Bible, I read that God loves a cheerful giver and I was so far from anything that vaguely resembled cheerful *or* giving. I fasted by praying. I fasted with pep talks. I fasted by reading spiritual growth books. I fasted with other people for support. The overbearing taunt that the soul is willing but the flesh is weak persisted. I finally waved the white surrender flag on this food fight. I needed to bind my wounds from the battlefield.

Friday rolled around and a friend asked what revelations my fasting experience had shown so far. Instead of regurgitating a litany about this self-inflicted martyrdom, I asked if he'd share his insight on asceticism (if we were playing Scrabble, asceticism would be worth 16 points on the board. Fasting, the plebian word for asceticism would have a mere 11 points. I digress).

My friend, Jared, shed invaluable light about fasting benefits. For him, he chose Friday as a natural fasting day since it is recognized in the Christian culture as the day Jesus was crucified. Jared explained that on Friday mornings, he asks God to give him extra strength to fully appreciate the sacrifice Jesus made on the cross. If the fasting is especially difficult one day, Jared looks at a cross and realizes that anything he would endure that day pales in comparison to the crucifixion. Eeks! My ears took a conviction blow, yet I pressed Jared for his strategy in physically functioning without food.

He said that if fasting waylaid him to the point of not fulfilling his vocation as a husband, a father, or a teacher, God doesn't desire that. He shared other strategies including when he was physically too worn-out to function at a level that would cause God to smile, he'd have a bowl of oatmeal or a piece of toast without toppings. He gained enough nutrition to maintain focus through the fast, but also acknowledged his fasting process through not indulging in butter, cinnamon, or honey that he'd ordinarily use in oatmeal or toast.

Jared also taught that fasting does not have to be limited to food. Some days, he takes a cooler shower with lower water pressure as physical sacrifice for people who don't have warm running water. Other days, he sleeps without a pillow to remind himself some people sleep on park benches or under a bridge. Jared shared sacrificial examples of discipline such as not allowing himself to murmur or complain; taking time to write support cards to people who need an emotional boost; volunteering time when his calendar is full instead of waiting for a more convenient window of time; giving to charity from his living expense budget instead of cash overflow (if there is such a thing). He reminded me that fasting is not about feelings. Some days, he is significantly moved by the Spirit to fast, others days he's lacking wholehearted devotion. His focus remains on regularly disciplining the body and acknowledging that God is the higher power.

Jared's perception renewed my clarity and offered a much-needed dose of encouragement. Instead of one long food fasting day, I looked for small daily fasts, using some of Jared's examples and incorporating disciplines of my own. While I ran, I took inventory of what potential challenges my day might bring. Instead of dreading, mustering, murmuring, bracing, or fussing my day away, I chose a fast that would match that possible obstacle. With proactive awareness, the figurative spear in my side and virtual crown of thorns was lifted.

I now choose to view fasting as a probortunity. Probortunity is a word one of my professors made up when she faced adversity. She said that on any level of annoyance, she defined probortunity as: "a problem with a chosen opportunity for me to solve it in a brighter, more optimistic way"

Days present various probortunities and I continue taking and making strides in fasting with positive momentum. The process of sacrificial discipline has been far from life in the fast lane, but I stretch toward a forward-moving motion. Instead of anticipating fasting as a force to be reckoned with, I climb the mountain with expectation that each step draws me closer to amazing scenery at the summit.

That amazing scenery includes gifts of achievement, confidence, courage, invigoration, and yes, sometimes a perceptional breakthrough. I am a work in progress.

NO SUCH THING AS A FREE LUNCH

I continue to learn from the fasting process. I have greater understanding of there is no such thing as a free lunch. I wanted to more willingly sacrifice when outreaches presented themselves, during times when it may be inconvenient to me. I was enthusiastic to give my surplus of time, extra money, or when virtual gushes of generosity wind blew around my heart. I desired to be a consistently charitable servant. God responded to this desire by presenting an opportunity one afternoon when I was driving home from work. I had about an hour commute and was eager to get dinner on the table and take an evening walk with my husband.

As I turned off the highway, a man with a cardboard sign stood at the ramp. His face was flushed from high humidity, his pants were at least two sizes too large for his frail frame, and his face was scruffy with salt and peppered stubble. Living in a city of 360,000 and at a peak interstate exchange, I'd see plenty of people holding cardboard signs. To some people, I shelled out a dollar or two if the light change took longer than expected. At other times I purposely veered toward the lane furthest from that person to avoid their hopeful stare. My generosity depended on my mood and judgment call, not necessarily an automatic outpouring to match a person's need. I was still in the honeymoon phase of understanding fasting and discipline, so I promptly decided to drive home to pick up our son and get some food for this man near the interstate. I wanted

Todd to experience outreach at a young age, to plant an awareness seed that grew beyond his current backyard view.

Todd gave a roll-the-middle-school-eye response when I got home and told him we were going on a spur-of-the-moment mission trip. He wanted details about what I was planning to do and his role in this spontaneous operation. He bristled, mainly because he didn't want to be interrupted in the middle of a video game. He defended his halfhearted response: "Mom, you can't help every homeless person on the interstate." I verified this truth and reminded Todd that this person was within a mile of our home and we needed to promptly take action. He dug in his heels, growing more agitated: "How do you know this guy is even homeless? He could just be lazy and not want to work." I retorted that it wasn't up to us to determine if his tattered cardboard sign was authentic. From his comfortable, climate controlled couch, Todd anchored his stance: "What if he tries to beat you up or something?" I appealed to his male ego and stated that rationale made it imperative that he came along to defend me if something went haywire when I gave this man food. I expected the supersized- teenage-head-toss-eye roll- lumber off-the couch-mumble-under-the-breath but he relented. I grabbed quick edibles from the pantry, a bottle of water, napkins, plastic ware, and we jumped in the car and drove to deliver this goody bag.

I used the dusky drive to the interstate to talk to Todd about the importance of this mother-son mission trip, the importance of non-judgmental giving, and probably a plethora of motherly knock-your-socks- off advice as we drove to feed this roadside man. We reached the interstate and the man was sweatier and more worn down than when I saw him thirty minutes prior. I parked the car and asked Todd to wait (with car doors locked…my sudden generosity surge didn't stomp out basic precautions). Still dressed in my work slacks, blazer, and pumps, I high- legged through thigh level scratchy grass, dodging sandburs. It was literally a field trip to reach this man, but I wanted to parent by example, teaching Todd to give even when it's not conveniently logical.

Any false sense of pride was extinguished when I got closer to this man. I held out the bag in front of me as if to show him I wasn't some professionally dressed woman schlepping through an interstate field to exchange greetings. I was about ten feet from him when he cursed and shouted: "God Dammit! Everyone today keeps trying to give me just *food*! I need *money*! I have bills to pay and food won't pay my bills!" I wilted from his fiery response and drew back my outstretched hand clutching the food bag. I froze, caught in a cross-fire between setting down the bag and running away, or retaliating while I carried the bag back to the car. He disengaged eye contact and went back to watching passing cars while I contemplated my next move. I walked away, bag in my hand when he suddenly hollered, "Hey lady, I'm sorry. I'm just having a really bad day. I'll take the food." I quickly took it back to him and mumbled a hurried good luck.

I returned to the car with my clothing sandbur-free, but my humility stitches were embedded with briars and brambles. Todd asked why the man got so angry and the lesson proved two-fold. I originally gave the food with a pure heart but my prideful agenda tried to steal God's show. I wanted Todd to see my willingness to step out of my comfort zone to meet others' needs. I wanted to prove that my actions and words aligned.

My second learning curve on the interstate loop wasn't a warm and fuzzy greeting card commercial, but it was important to be obedient to God's calling. I was to accomplish His will without assuming or anticipating the recipient's response. Just because God's assignment didn't match my hope of the outcomes, I was to respectfully obey His mission call.

After mental realignment, I gained traction in my earthly pilgrimage. I was not going to let one man's rough day deplete my eagerness to serve. I learned a valuable lesson about expecting lavish praise from the recipient and needing to move over so God got the limelight and glory.

To avoid becoming gun shy about future outreach, I looked for another service project. I needed to practice releasing personal expectations and demonstrate that one person's terse reaction wouldn't continue to dampen my budding servant heart.

With the next outreach, I enlisted Tig's assistance. Participating as a family would represent a unified serving body. This time, we were a team instead of me stepping out on a solo mission. This time, Todd was onboard to deliver sack lunches to each person holding a cardboard sign the Sunday following that interstate disconnection. In the past, we turned a semi-blind eye to many needy people. This sack lunch mission was a chance to improve our family vision.

Todd, Tig, and I went to the grocery store to buy food for 15 lunches. Each lunch included a peanut butter and jelly sandwich, bag of crackers, juice box, apple, and wrapped dessert. We turned our kitchen into a short-term assembly line and together we slathered peanut butter and jelly on bread and bagged lunches for 15 people.

There are two sides of town where we often saw people holding cardboard signs so we drove to those areas first. We drove through parking lots and alleys. Neither area had anyone standing by stop lights or dumpsters where we previously saw needy people. We headed toward the main interstate exchange, made a few circles around frequented exits, thinking we may have missed people when we drove that area the first time.

After three hours of driving, Tig was getting aggravated about our fuel usage for seemingly no purpose. Todd was in the backseat griping that we give up and go back home. I was determined that our family mission would not be thwarted so I asked Tig to drive downtown near the homeless shelters and give the lunches to people who looked like they most needed food. Tig reluctantly said he'd drive another ½ hour toward downtown, but felt too awkward walking up to a stranger and handing them a sack lunch. Todd, with his pre-teen wisdom, said by giving food to a random person, I was judging their need or even their desire to be helped.

My initial excitement and perseverance was waning. I questioned the purity of my motives. I silently asked God to send us people who needed meals. As we were driving downtown, the sky opened up to a downpour. Yes! The rain *had* to be God's positive recognition to my prayer. My interpretation of that cloudburst was how crucial our lunches became now that it was raining. Maybe the initial sunshine at the beginning of our mission trip was a test to see if we'd persist in a rainstorm.

With renewed spirit, I fully anticipated God showing us people huddled under bridges or crammed under a store awning seeking refuge from rain. Tig drove the truck down Martin Luther King Boulevard near housing projects; past the bus depot on Central Avenue; up and down 5th Avenue by the Salvation Army and a local mission. Nobody was on the streets. Not even one person was milling around the usual side streets. I echoed Tig & Todd's weariness and accepted their plea to go home with 15 uneaten, unshared lunches.

We each took a sack lunch as we headed out the door Monday morning (and Tuesday morning and Wednesday morning and…By Friday, with no packing lunch chores for the week, I had time to reflect on Sunday's attempted delivery drive. In jumping on my outreach bandwagon, I realize I may have jumped ahead of God's requests for that day. He may have had different plans for Tig and Todd's day. Instead of asking God how I could fit into His assignments, I assumed He'd adjust to my blueprints. From a motive standpoint, I'm not implying I did something sinful or corrupt, but our family outreach stemmed from *my* desire to serve others according to *my* schedule. I throttled ahead with *my* agenda before asking God what He wanted from our family's time.

I received a free tutorial about stopping to listen and hear God's ideas. I sometimes forget that the Lord's Prayer teaches "Thy will be done" not '*my* will be done'. I learned my own priceless lesson about embracing experiences as they evolve. I gained new comprehension about how the beauty of random acts of kindness stems from unexpected appreciation or surprises. There is a level of necessary planning to create positive activity. Handing over the keys to God and riding shotgun in His vehicle make my daily road trips smoother.

Within days of our family's city tour, I received confirmation of God's lesson. Diane Eble, author of *Abundant Gifts: A Daybook of Grace Filled Devotions*, featured 1 Kings 8:17-19 to explain

David's desire to build a temple to honor the Lord. The Lord told David his intentions were good but David was not the person assigned to that construction site. Instead, one of David's sons built the temple to honor God. Eble wrote: "Don't be discouraged if your good intentions don't always end up the way you envisioned them. Instead celebrate the ministry you do have and encourage your vision of great things. Perhaps God has placed a person in your life perfectly suited to see your ideas come to life."

That spiritual vitamin of reinforcement invited freedom to drop my gridlocked agenda and open the gates for daily surprises. Instead of bulldozing an enclosed tunnel to shuttle through my day, I created margins of space into a 24 hour block. I still work most efficiently and happily with planned intervals of what I consider productive time, but have shifted my mindset to allow wiggle room. I have a general blueprint of each day in mind, but now it includes larger places for God to add His windows of opportunity, knock down walls, and design colorful landscaping. I'm more eager to check in with the Universe's Master Designer and Architect before I open my tool box (or voice box)!

THIS LITTLE PIGGY WENT TO MARKET

From a broad perspective, I think many of us are in the marketing profession, no matter what educational degree or career path we pursued. Some of us market products. Some of us feature a behavior trait. Some of us showcase talents. We serve as individual billboards for the human condition. We each display a personal message center representing my values, beliefs, past experiences, and future aspirations. I'm a virtual road sign wherever my travels take me that day through words, actions, and facial expressions. My responses and reactions become a marquee. Many days, my "showroom floor" is inviting and welcoming. Other days, I'd rather hang a "gone fishing" sign around the time clock. At times, my job status yearns to scream, "Have a nice day… but somewhere else!" When I hit those icy personality patches in the "frozen food aisle", it's time to order myself a truckload of warmer energy.

I take state-of-mind inventory in my personal stockroom, scanning interactions between people in situations I face. For example, I remember a post office clerk being intentionally kind to every customer in their lengthy line. Or the gas station worker offering an enthusiastic greeting, even though I later found out he was working two jobs to meet the bills. Or the plumber who came to our house to fix a busted pipe on Christmas Eve while his family waited for him at home to open presents. Or the mom who divided a meal among her children and went hungry so her kids were fed. Whether it's a limelight, flashlight, or candle light, I have a choice to shine brightness into another person's life. Does my light have glow-in-the-dark intensity, or is my dimmer switch lending itself toward recall mode?

A friend, who was facing her cancer battle, had a unique way of defeating discouragement and negative thoughts during treatments. While she went through chemotherapy and radiation, people asked how she was feeling. She'd answer, "Tremendous, *and improving*!" Or, "Fantastic, *and improving*!" She said it was difficult enough to face physical cancer, but wasn't going to worsen her diagnosis by spreading spiritual cancer. Instead, she'd respond with a power adjective even when she felt weak. She has been cancer free for many years and still credits uplifting words that infused healing.

Similar to my return wave/smile response game on running routes, I observe group interactions then challenge myself to guess the direction of general dynamics. My only rule, with and for myself, is a black or white option. There may be unlimited "grey" layers within group communication, but I wager a guess using a black and white overview of the situation.

This game is a bit like a vision test when the eye exam room is dimly lit and the optometrist introduces your face to some 400 pound metal contraption. The doctor shines an image on the screen with the question, "can you see A or B better?" You answer, hoping you either chose correctly or the doctor doesn't judge you based on your eyesight, or lack thereof. The doctor gives no indication about how close you came to the answer with 50/50 odds. He or she adjusts the lens, shows the same screen, and asks again, "does A or B look clearer?" You go through this battery of tests a few times until you tell the doctor when you get the sharpest vision. After several ticks on that robot looking concoction, I'm concerned the optometrist will fill my vision prescription with a seeing-eye dog. Any time I can incorporate a canine into my life, it's a terrific story in my eyes.

Back to my guess-the-interaction game. This sample comes from a recent experience of waiting in a bank line. Just as the bank doors open on a Tuesday morning after a three-day holiday weekend, a customer watches for a teller to open her window, frequently exhaling while he waits. He loudly announces he's closing all accounts. I picture my go-to reaction if I was in that bank teller's position. From a virtual vision exam chair, my "A" game lens defaults to a clear screen of gentle kindness. My "B" game lens does a squint-strain-my-chin-forward-to-reach-beyond-the-veins-popping-in-my-neck lens as I interact with that irate customer.

As a third party observer, I determine if my focus would be life-giving or knock-the-wind-out-of-someone's-irate-sails. With both responses, I'm either marketing myself as a billboard, lit with hope filled messages, or a peeling paint sign that advertises "better-go-out-of-business." I have the power to build or erode, to positively affect or infect interactions.

How do I show up for every-day life? If my work day resembles a forgotten Oreo cookie at the bottom of a milk glass, why do I expect others to retrieve my soggy crumbs? How is it acceptable that my audience's virtual fingers have to fish to the bottom of the glass to grasp cookie mush just because *I'm* struggling? I'm not advocating phony smiles, false authenticity, or assuming I fully understand another person's struggles, but when have I accepted threadbare job performance? Long-term respected people become well-known through several baby steps of excellence in smaller roles.

I sometimes wonder how my life would look like if I worked a high profile position, spending much public time in the limelight. If I was an actress, musician, or government official, would I approach those professions the same way I conduct my occupation as author and life coach? Would I enthusiastically perform a concert or television broadcast with a smile every day, ready to set the world on fire just because I was a well-known newscaster or band member?

For instance, Bruce Springsteen. In the music world, Springsteen is known as "The Boss." I've dreamed of seeing him perform live. What if I saved money, camped overnight for tickets, invited friends, planned an entire evening around the Bruce Springsteen experience. He's performed thousands of concerts to sold-out crowds. He's had amazing reviews and I anticipate a powerfully impressive show.

However, what if on the night of my long awaited concert, The Boss showed up for work and just wasn't feeling it? That somehow, for my magical castle in the sky evening, he happened to be so sick of his job that he was ready to hang it up? Visualize him stepping onto the stage an hour late, unenthusiastically singing his opening tune followed by a dramatic yawn during the second song. The band plays a few notes to introduce the next song and Springsteen rolls his eyes mid-verse as if to say, "no, not again!" He limply strums his guitar, laxly looking around without acknowledging the crowd and sings with mediocrity at best. The crowd (especially me, me me!) expects professionalism, high energy, and satisfaction. Springsteen's audience doesn't anticipate filling out a customer complaint card or posting bad ratings after his show.

Maybe on the night of this hypothetical not-so-dreamy-concert, Springsteen's tour bus broke down on the way to the auditorium. Maybe the band was weary from restless sleep. Perhaps Bruce and his wife had a spat just before he went on tour. He may have been fighting flu and would rather have been home soaking in a warm tub. The empathy card isn't the first draw of the deck when we consider lackluster performance. Personal expectations trump. Whatever circumstances a spotlight performer experiences before going on stage, ticket holders presume the show will be top notch. Despite weaknesses or setbacks limelight workers experience prior to show time, most times they hike up their big boy or big girl britches. They deliver a polished performance whether that concert is free or high ticket price because their audience looks forward to professionalism.

I'm guessing Bruce Springsteen's audience would probably understand a less than stellar performance if he talked about his pre-show tribulations. Nonetheless, the crowd would likely be disappointed if he displayed less than what he was capable. Similarly, I consider it my responsibility (and desire on most days) to show up for my "audience" at my best, despite circumstances or feelings. I don't (or shouldn't) expect the gas station attendant, other interstate drivers, husband, son, co-workers, my dogs, mail carrier, or hair dresser to bear the brunt of my frustrations. If a 'less than attentive driver' pulls in front of me their 'less than attentive action doesn't justify my all-day rant wherever I go for the rest of the day. Just because morning preparation time flies by and I'm running behind doesn't endorse my frustration on whomever or whatever crosses my path (even if that indulgence is tempting).

Hours or sometimes days can be an uphill climb to temper unglued emotions. Sometimes I have to apply inner caulk to weakened gaps in my foundation. Those cracks draw me toward God as I seek His repair to my sensitive view of certain situations. I need His eyes to see a clearer picture. The ideal "Guess How I Would Respond" game requires routine vision check-ups. In looking at interactions, does the A or B lens on the life-size screen appear more in focus? I want to be the kind of person someone recalls as "that lady who was graceful even when circumstances were gritty."

MY OWN CHEERING SECTION

I'm writing this segment a week before Super Bowl. The chatter about snacks, football parties, the team most likely to win, and commercial recaps from past Super Bowls is rampant. The hot air output is enough to melt the ice on the roads. This is the week where I practice self-discipline in voicing my opinion about the football industry being over-rated. Football season seems to last eleven months.

I haven't determined the specific reason for my lack of enthusiasm for ball sports. Perhaps it's because I'm not gifted in hand-eye coordination. Maybe I secretly wish cross country running fans would draw the crowds and enthusiasm as traditional sports. At running events, I yearn for elaborate concession stands and toilet facilities that are offered in many other sports' venues. I haven't taken the interest or time to learn about game objectives so I'm often startled by sudden uproars, whoops, and outbursts from cheering (or jeering) fans.

To proactively combat football season woes, I incorporated Sunday afternoons from August through January for leisure reading. All week, I anticipated a three hour block during the 1:00 game time to read and nap. I grabbed a book, warm beverage, fleece blanket, soft thick socks, and head for the den. Just as I settled into where I left off in the story line from last Sunday, it happened…

Out of the blue, I heard verbal thunder. "Come on, come on, come on!!!! Get 'em, get, get, get, GET him!" Tig and Todd were yelling at the TV, not the protagonist in my current novel. I braced for another bolt of their couch coaching. When I heard both guys exhale and sit heavily back into their chairs, I resumed the pre-outburst plotline. Within a few pages, a sound resembling a rabbit caught in a bear trap came from the den (the downstairs den, not a grizzly's abode). "Uhhhhhh! What are you THINKING ref?" Since I didn't hear the ref's response, I presumed the game official wasn't stopping the game to share his thoughts with my husband. All was silent. It appeared safe to read for comprehension until a few seconds of a page flip when Todd roared, "Goll, how many more times are you going to run that same play?"

This volley between grappling for story content and the guys' sudden outbursts continued. By the end of three hours my literary "holy hour" turned into something less than holy (and most of the holies ended with words that may cause a fumble). Sunday rolled around again. Instead of my read time, I went for a run while the guys' team played. When the game was over, I was eager to celebrate literacy in sweet peaceful silence. In my master game plan, I didn't factor overtime because in the sport of cross country running, it isn't common to register for a 10K race only to be told at mile 6.2 that runners need to finish with the half-marathoners. I realized the juiciest plot in a book wouldn't hold my concentration during this extended-dance-version of the game. Overtime only increased the tense-off-the-couch-eeks-my-pants-are-on-fire-I-think-I'll-leap-up-and-scream-at-the-players-on-TV moments.

Finally, after another verbal power surge, I stomped to the living room, "Guys! You *do* realize that no matter *how* loud you scream at that television, the players can't hear you, right?" Simultaneously, with mischievous grins, Tig and Todd answered, "*We* think they *can*!" Todd reasoned first downs only happen *because* he yells. Tig insisted there have been more total running yards *because* he loudly encourages the players. The guys defended their sideline coaching by saying how yelling during a game improves communication among men. They sheepishly winked at each other because they hear my perpetual quest for two way communication. They promised to minimize noise levels so I could go back to reading.

The following weeks of football season, Tig and Todd remained courteous in toning down their animated coaching. A few times they even shushed each other during a game upset or exciting play to remind each other I was reading. It would be perfectly quaint to end our football frenzy story with "and they all lived happily ever after." After a few weeks of their marked courtesy, the season neared playoffs and their original method of male communication took over. The guys went back to pseudo coaching and I once again read sentences multiple times to decipher a smidgen of story development.

Through wisdom, or possibly a hint of passive-aggressiveness, I approached the following game day with an attitude that if I couldn't beat 'em, join 'em. I'd match my book reading with the intensity of their animated game watching. I had enough sense to use my jaded technique during commercials or duller segments of the game. During a first quarter commercial, I suddenly let out a gigantic whoop from my reading chair. Tig bolted upstairs with concern. He asked why I yelled. Without looking up from my book, I nonchalantly answered, "I was excited to read." He rolled his eyes and mumbled his way back downstairs. I listened for the next commercial and then shrieked, "No way! This can't be happening!" Tig and Todd both came running to see me sitting in the comfy chair, wide eyed at the page in front of me. He raised his eyebrows, "What happened now?" With extreme hype, I answered, "I thought for *sure* the murder evidence was hidden in the library, but the detectives found it behind the *dance studio*, which made it look like the studio owner was the killer. Someone framed her!" The guys rolled their eyes and Tig assured Todd, "that was your Mom's lame attempt to mock our team support." They insisted that they aren't *that* over-the-top in their cheering.

I admit a bit of guilty delight in commentating and shouting play-by-play responses at my book. I cheered the investigators, shouted at the antagonists. I booed the timing of events that hindered police from arriving at the crime scene and jumped up and down with a victory dance when the mystery unraveled. The guys weren't impressed by my play-by-play recap, but I found a new layer of fun in reading. . I revert to the commentating strategy whenever the guys "television coach." I match commentary for *whatever* I'm doing to the volume and intensity of their sports' outbursts.

For the following paragraph, you may want to use a fast-speaking-enthusiastic-radio-sounding-voice. If you wish to continue your radio voice to finish this book, that could add an entertaining twist to your reading.

"Folks, thank you for coming out this afternoon to watch a heavy showdown between woman and vacuum cleaner. We check in now on the competition already in progress between female and electronic beast...
She slowly makes her way to the broom closet, gaining momentum as she nears the dust sucking machine. She stops at the doorway, checking to make sure no other family member sees her plan of attack. She notices an opening in human floor traffic and wham! Off she goes, flings open the door, grabs the vacuum cleaner by the neck and yanks it from behind the doorway. Looking behind her to make sure nobody is going to steal her show she plugs the prongs into the outlet. She pushes the "on" button and whoa! The vacuum comes alive! This woman is on fire tonight! All the power cleans she's done to prepare for this moment are really paying off! No man can measure up to this lady's athletic strength

as she not only pushes that vacuum but pulls it as well. She truly is a force to be reckoned with. Wait, wait, wait! What do we have in the middle of this playing field? One of her elderly dogs has executed a sneak attack and planted his resting body on the floor right in front of the vacuum! Will she call a time out? Will there be a penalty flag on the dog? How is this woman going to stop the monumental force of her arms and shoulders to avoid a major upset in this cleaning mission? The mental discipline she's developed through years of running comes to a head right in front of our eyes, folks. She focuses. She squints. She isn't letting up on the gap that is decreasing between dog and vacuum. Just before the clock runs out, she stiff arms the vacuum, narrowly missing the unsuspecting dog and makes a break for the other side of the room. The crowd is on their feet (insert a little cheer noise for bonus sound effects). What an upset! She powers the vacuum to the end zone of the room and the fans go wild! Christina jumps on the back of the sofa, doing a victory dance, show-boating a hard earned victory. The floor is clean, the dog is saved, and Christina adds yet another jewel to crown her vacuuming career. Fans! This event is what you would definitely call a "clean sweep!" Tune in next week folks when we watch this same woman face a streak-free window washing extravaganza. Now back to your regularly scheduled program, "Agitation Meets Proactive Humor."

THE WIND BENEATH MY WING

I was contracted by a weekly paper to write uplifting from-the-heart stories. The column's purpose was to add lighthearted reading for the small town publication. I often used part of my running time to brainstorm ideas for that writing assignment. This is a sampling from the column *Quibbles and Bits* that readers commented on most frequently. The following was titled *The Wind Beneath My Wing*.

As I got off the plane after an intense work week, I didn't have my usual anticipation of briskly walking to the receiving terminal. This time, I wouldn't be scanning the crowd to find my husband Tig and our son Todd rushing into my arms for a shower of hugs and kisses. I knew I wouldn't have their helpful hands to schlep luggage, carry-on bag, and the portable classroom I used for training seminars. When I got home, I dreaded the house being as quiet as a Monday morning church. Not even our Lhasa Apso would be at the doorway impersonating the friendliest Wal-Mart greeter.

These tears were usually reserved for the flights *away* from home. This flight back home was so much different. Two days earlier, Tig and Todd had driven 14 hours to visit my father-in-law who was battling Huntington's Disease. They would be gone three more days and after a long week, this extra stretch of time apart seemed an eternity. As I walked past other travelers reuniting with their waiting parties, I kept a stiff upper lip. My focus on fighting back tears in public suddenly got directed toward a military family. How often did *their* family need to say goodbye? How many times did they get separated from each other for several *months*? Despite my attempted optimistic overdose, my spirit remained sedated under the medication of sadness as I walked to the airport parking lot.

I balanced all four bags between my shoulders, hip, and arm, teetering my way toward the parking lot. It was dark, cold and somewhat eerie that late at night. I anticipated the relief I'd feel when I could finally set down my heavy luggage. I walked around Level One of the parking lot, searching for my car among rows and rows of other cars. I had written Level One on the back of my parking ticket when I arrived at the airport the prior week to remember where my car was parked. With forced confidence, I reassured myself that my parking space was nearby. I made a second pass among the aisles, looking more intently for my red Sunfire.

A man I had not noticed before suddenly started walking toward me, a certain smile covering his face. I tried straightening up under the weight of the luggage, giving the impression that I was self-assured, less weary, and larger than my 5'3, 110-pound frame. This man continued his intentional pace in my direction. Although he didn't necessarily look dangerous, I was cautious because it was nearly midnight, I was alone and this big city parking lot was not my number one choice for an evening walk. I composed a stern facial expression to imply strength, despite my trembling arms and burning shoulders from lugging a week's worth of cargo through the dimly lit lot.

The man squinted as he got closer and stated, "You seem upset." Lying, I answered, "No, just a long work week." He smiled, matched my pace, and opened his winter jacket lapel to reveal his airport employee identification badge. I gave a laugh of relief and began babbling, "Actually I've been trudging around for almost half an hour trying to find my car that I parked in Level One last week, my arms are so tired, my husband and our son usually are with me to help, and now I'm worried that my car may have been stolen or towed. Plus it's late and I don't want to call anyone to give me a ride." I inhaled deeply after my panicky onslaught and glanced at this innocent target who just absorbed a verbal assault from my harried explanation. His retirement aged eyes grew animated as he patiently waited for me to take another breath. He said, "Ma'am, we're standing in the short-term parking lot. Your car is probably in the long-term lot on Level One. Let me carry some of that luggage and we'll find that car of yours."

We walked around until we found my Sunfire right where I had parked it over a week ago. The man loaded everything in the car without further questions or implied judgment about my frazzled sense. I reached for my purse to offer him a tip but he insistently declined. I explained how much I appreciated him and how much it meant that he helped me at a time when I needed it so much. In a grandfatherly way he answered, "Sometimes the best part of this gig is not the financial piece. It's about doing parts of the job that are *not* written in my formal duty description." With another gentle reassuring smile, he directed me toward the closest cashier line so I could get out of the parking lot quickly.

Since this stranger wouldn't accept money in exchange for my appreciation, I asked him how I could repay him for his generosity. He simply said, "Say a prayer for me." He had no specific request, no detailed need, just that basic request. I asked for his name so I would know what name to write in my prayer journal. He replied, "The name's Raymond ma'am."

As Raymond walked away, I recognized that a part of my family was right there in name and spirit. Raymond is my brother's name. My brother was named after my grandfather Raymond who was killed in a car accident when my dad was 17 years old. I never met my grandfather, yet I felt the presence of a guardian angel in Raymond. My drive home was more peaceful than I anticipated. I was alone when I walked into the house that night, but I wasn't lonely. Raymond had been a wind beneath my wing, and this certain wing had nothing to do with the airplane that flew me home.

ON THE JOB TRAINING

I save humorous topics to jog my mind when I run longer distances. The comic relief distracts my thoughts from the pain of enduring that last leg of a lengthy course. Jobs offer an enormous arena for comical interaction. I used to joke with my coworkers about writing a book about our workday and to offset publishing costs, I'd charge people to stay *out* of the story. The following blips are some of my favorite smiles to offset the sweat equity during extensive miles.

As a former regional trainer of a weight loss clinic, I was doing a walk-through of the centers in my territory. One center's inspirational quote by the scale read, "There aren't enough crutches in the world to hold up all your lame excuses."

At the same company, we had a counselor who used words out of context. During medical history screenings, instead of asking if a client had high cholesterol, she asked if the person had high collateral. She asked another client if he was hypochondriac instead of if he was hypoglycemic.

A male job candidate came to our office to fill out a job application. The staff was on alert because our business historically attracted more female applicants. The job application was typically completed within 10-15 minutes. After a half-hour, the hiring manager asked this candidate if he had any questions about the application. He replied he only had a few more lines to fill out. It seemed odd he had taken nearly double the usual amount of time to finish the form. It was even more unusual that he added 20 more minutes to finish the application. When he brought the clipboard to the front desk, he said he didn't think there would be so many questions and because it had taken so long to fill out the application he couldn't stay to interview. He apologized for leaving before he could talk to a manager but assured us he'd call the next day to reschedule an interview. When he left, we were curious about why it took this man nearly an hour to complete what we thought was a fairly simple process. The manager took the clip board to her office to review his responses and soon we heard her belly laughing all the way down the hallway. This man not only completed the application, he filled out two *identical* weight loss *client* questionnaires. Since the "potential weight loss client" questionnaires were tucked under the employment applications, this job seeker filled out every page on that clipboard.

The manager shared her sources of laughter from this candidate's job application/weight loss questionnaire combo:

Q: How long have you been thinking about losing weight?
A: I do not need to lose any weight.

Q: What made you choose today to come to our center?
A: I needed to apply for a job.

Q: How has your family supported your weight loss efforts?
A: They support me in my job search and if I had to lose weight, they'd support me there too.

Q: Tell us about your current eating habits.
A: Breakfast, lunch, dinner, midnight snack if I'm hungry.

Q: How committed are you to losing weight?
A: Not very, I just want this job.

No further questions were needed. We freed him up to pursue career opportunities in other businesses.

DELIVERY CHARGE

Another classic story is delivered from my time working at Pizza Hut. This was during the 80's when only a few pizza places offered delivery service. It was a stormy Saturday evening and for some reason rain tends to invite more people to order pizza. I'm not sure if rain is to pizza cravings as cold weather is to mashed potato hankerings, but that night we were intensely stretched to stay ahead of all the pizza orders.

The dine-in traffic was heavy, carry out orders were abundant, and the phone was ringing off the hook. We stayed open until 1:00 Friday and Saturday evenings and by the time closing duties were finished, it was always well after 2:00 before employees could go home. We braced ourselves for an even later departure that night. As the orders continued in monsoon proportion, pizza wait time was increasing and patience was decreasing. It rained outside, but a virtual storm brewed inside the restaurant as employees hollered at each other to move faster, pay attention, and get out of each other's way. The clock finally struck 12:30 and we knew we were on the homeward stretch.

The coworker on phone duty was weary from three lines bombarding him with new orders, checking on existing orders, questions about coupons and meal deals. He fielded complaints in between reassuring customers we were doing the best we could. His temperament was wearing thin so when the phone rang at 12:30, he answered the call with flippant irritability. The person on the other end asked if we still delivered that late at night. My ordinarily professional coworker echoed the pizza customer's question, "do we *deliver*?" Sure we'll deliver! How far apart are your contractions"?

I'm hard-pressed to envision that caller's facial expression after my coworker's response. However, I did see our manager's facial expression which led to intense words of fellowship with my exhausted snappy coworker.

TIDAL WAVE

Shortly after hearing the song, *Tidal Wave* at church, I was reminded of prior summers when we bought season passes to a tidal wave park. In my mind, I'm floating along on that flimsy but strong pool raft, anticipating the warning buzzer that soon the tidal waves will intensify. I grip the raft a bit tighter, waiting for the nervous anticipated thrill. Waves rush, fellow swimmers scream with excitement, and we cling to our mats, working to ride the waves without being sucked under the current. Even though the slapping and surging water is extreme, there's an underlying security that the water park control tower will return those waves to a floating peaceful state. Part of our peace also comes from knowing that if a swimmer *would* go under water, a lifeguard would rush to their aid.

In current life, we face a discouraging diagnosis, an addicted family member, a physical deformity, a kidnapped child, a fallen soldier, a shooting. We may face tidal waves. Without the warning timer, we often do not know when a wave will come. Unlike the mechanical box control, we cannot set the wave's pressure or determine how long the wave will last. During waves, we gulp air and rest when we can, not knowing the duration of the severity. As tension rises and protective walls threaten to plummet, we seek to crawl onto our mat in the fetal position until the engulfing waves no longer pose a hazard.

That tidal wave parallel offered me comfort. God offered additional revelations about that visual. We *don't* know when those waves are coming, but He is our raft (and much sturdier than that wobbly nap mat included in the park admission ticket). He serves a dual purpose in keeping us afloat *and* anchored in His hand.

Another eureka layer to that revelation is we *do* have a perpetual lifeguard. The original Water Walker can perfectly scoop us out of danger. At times, He *allows* storms of varying intensity. I got a tsunami of a lesson when I was in my 30's and learned that God doesn't *cause* turbulence. He *allows* whirlpools to invite us to swim to His shore for strength and protection from dangerous waters. He doesn't order chaos so He can create some type of cynical job security for Himself. Just as a swimmer needs a strong muscle to counter the current, an individual needs powerful heart muscle to grow character. Whether it's the waiting room or the weight room, we have His raft and anchor. We receive eternal salvation at baptism, the ultimate water park! Our Raft and Anchor are much lighter and easier to fit in our pockets than a physical raft and anchor.

Just as tidal wave parks close during winter, overnight, or severe storms, we are positioned to pause for a set time. We need a break to rub aloe on our sunburns, take deep breaths free of the daily wave torment, and rest our muscles. During that floating time, there is still moving current, but a gentler pace allows us to relax our shoulders and chest. It's a time to virtually sit on a towel, listen to life giving music, and feed on written nourishment. "Be still and know that I am God" (Ps. 46:10 NIV) invites us to play with fellow swimmers, nap in the warm sun, and peacefully reflect on how God carries us through the storm. Calm water seasons encourage us to sharpen ourselves with new skills to prepare for the next wave. Fortunately, our universal Lifeguard is on duty 24/7. Hold onto our Lifeguard, His raft, His anchor!

SCALING BACK

As a runner, I'm conscious about nutrition, recognizing wholesome foods produce a stronger run. I've indulged in some eat-like-crud days, only to come back from a run feeling poisoned and bogged down from sugar or fat-laden carbs. Nutrition labels expose nearly everything that goes into a product, whether I can pronounce it or not. A side note: a glaring nemesis was born after I read the label of a Hostess cherry pie, one of my staples in high school.

The world offers me every tool, gimmick, and resource to keep fit. In addition to nutrition labels, we have calorie counters, pedometers, scales to measure body mass index of muscle to fat. Doctors order blood tests to check thyroid and kidney functions, sodium and blood sugar levels. Greater education about nutrition is vital, but some of this knowledge has become a nail in my obsessive coffin. When the label crazed bandwagon passed by, I jumped on. I began calculating calories, sugar grams, amounts of pre-loaded salt in 'health' food, and a plethora of measurable ways to streamline my diet.

I used more running time tracking nutrition instead of inviting less constricting thoughts to flow. Instead of appreciating the way my body moved, I beat it up as I started paying more attention to how I could eat cleaner. I fed a growing obsession that I'd run faster or with more stamina if I ate more of this, less of that. Instead of new thoughts, funny stories, ways to add value to people's lives, or smiling at others, I was now running with anxiety concocted from self-imposed perfect health modifications.

The pleasure of running started to fade because I fell into a pit where thoughts resembled a mathematical or scientific formula. It's a sanity killer for a creative writer to use running time to process nutritional ratios over and over and over and over again. I needed to jump off this mental treadmill. It was time to retrain my brain and turn to free flow thinking, to marry nutritional knowledge with soul health. This body-soul combination was similar to sending my spirit into a mystical scale to evaluate its composition.

Each week I wrote "What's Eating You?" at the top of my mileage log. Questions included: "How am I digesting self-talk? Do my words convert to fat or build lean muscle? Is my sense of humor too salty? Are my compliments full of natural sugar or do they resemble artificial sweetener? Do my actions create positive movement in my heart? Do I use my conscience filter to flush out poisonous relationships? Would my life's priorities make it to a list for "Best Uses for 24 Hours?"

These answers aren't weighed on a scale and their results aren't scanned neatly into my health chart. They are stored in journals where I reference them in the X-ray of my mind. When I'm mentally and emotionally toxic, I write my pain sources as a sweat equity workout. I put pen to paper to seek answers, vent, rewrite, vent some more, reassess, repeat any part of the process until I have fully released whatever causes a volatile response. Scrap paper, pen, shredder, and time are my four effective natural cleansers from the inside out. Organic, 100% wholesome, a gritty texture at times, mostly a nutty flavor, always home grown from my heart!

A LAB TEST

One evening, I watched James, our black lab puppy, paw at his tennis ball that had rolled underneath a kitchen chair. He repeatedly stretched his "arm" to reach the ball and kept coming up short. He tried sticking his head under a chair rung and moved his neck in various positions to nudge his nose toward that elusive lime green prize. He batted, lunged, and stared the ball down for at least ten minutes as if he'd retrieve it through osmosis. I was inspired by his tenacity and patience. He didn't bark or growl, he simply persevered. James exhausted every canine option but quitting was not his choice. I needed to move the chair so he could claim his well-earned trophy.

Like a lab, I sometimes approach life like James pursued his tennis ball. I try different methods, crane my neck and search for new angles to reach a desired solution. I'm willing to endure but also grateful to whoever lifts or carry a burden. Sometimes it's simply someone offering a new method to approach the situation. A compassionate person sees my struggle, understands the need, and moves my chair, so to speak.

I wonder how long James would have persisted to rescue that ball from under the chair. Would something else have captured his attention? He was about 60 pounds and capable of moving the chair himself, but he didn't realize that. Would his level of frustration have driven him to use his own strength to gain that ball?

My prayer life falls into a similar scenario. Recently, I listened to *Experiencing God* by Henry and Richard Blackaby. In that powerful teaching, the authors talk about how we often want an assignment without first developing the relationship with the Creator of Assignments. The teaching discusses our love for a ministry without first loving the Master of Ministry. We want to move into activity, to have our purpose given to us, to be fit for a larger assignment or a different mission yet we don't take time to seek God's preparation.

I pray for breakthrough, I ask God for answers. I want a drive- thru revelation but instead of waiting it out, I'd rather walk it out. Walking seems more productive because there's something physical to show for the effort. Waiting is... Well, waiting. Waiting is just that. Waiting. Ironically, wait is a verb, yet when I am waiting, there is nothing that represents action to me. That patience in waiting requires a heart transplant. I'm prone to just want a quick surgical bypass to reach the healing fast track. I want to speed past transitional recovery time and hurry onto therapy. Just fix whatever it is!

James, through his own "lab test", taught me persistent faithfulness in his attempts to dislodge that ball. He did his part and I was compassionately moved and able to do my part in moving the chair.

God responds in a similar way. He chooses to use me as part of His earthly plan. He places a plan in front of me and then invites me to trust Him, to keep trying (without growling or barking). Each time I work toward His perfect plan, I gain wisdom and strength. Ultimately it's He who aligns the best-for-me pieces of His plan and then moves my chair at His perfect time. Sometimes He allows me to keep trying, sometimes He waits for me to ask, and sometimes He makes me simply wait. With God as my Physician and me as a compliant patient, I'm progressing toward healthier "lab" results!

QUIET TIME

The majority of my creative notions are birthed from when I am most still. This isn't necessarily an off-the-chart shocker, but I realize that sometimes a bulk of my everyday battle stems from lack of solitude.

I recognize that not only do I want, but need my morning block of time to brainstorm and talk to God. Sometimes it's difficult to settle into a space of stillness because I'm eager to rattle off my agenda then hit the ground running. In a past journal entry, I found a description of how I was showing up for quiet time. I wrote, "I'm struggling to get quiet because I know our time (mine and God's together) is shorter than usual this morning. I feel like I'm wrestling porcupines. My mind is flooded with so much to wrap my head around. My insides resemble a shaken soda bottle. Instead of just allowing my internal fizz to settle before reading today's devotional, I'm rambling and scrambling to read as much as possible and gulping what I can."

Interestingly, time redemption transpires when I take two minutes to simply sit before I read or journal. Those 120 seconds *seem* like 30 minutes to wait for my soulful shaken ginger ale to defizz, but it pays nearly immediate dividends. I'll quietly say something to the effect of "Lord, I'm lacking concentration. Please calm me. I'll wait here silently until I receive your peace before I open any of my quiet time books so I can better hear from you." The tension subsides as if God reaches down and gently unscrews the cap to release mental fizz.

Instead of ignoring or fighting my distractions, I've found that calling out restlessness sends it packing much sooner. It's like a virtual tattle tale on the chaos threatening my quiet time playground. I use a monotone as a calming mechanism to say: "Right now, I'm worry that during this quiet moment I'm going to lose track of time and be late for x. Agitation isn't going to get me to x sooner and stuffing this concern will manifest in a different way. I direct all anxiety to make a beeline so peace can enter my spirit."

Taking control over my wayward thoughts requires practice. Initially, managing emotions feels like riding a unicycle, but I'm empowered when peaceful balance replaces clumsiness. Verbally assessing my frequently changing feelings deters me from giving in to my natural hurried panic. In runner's terms, positive emotional steeping is like a slow steady distance pace. A negative caffeine jolt of energy can become a sprint induced hamstring tear to the soul.

The difference between sprinting and steeping was further revealed on my commute. I wanted to stay on the mountain summit of fresh spiritual perception instead of driving to the foothills of my job. To write this on paper sounds elementary to me, but the earned wisdom was equivalent to a college degree. I realized I was storing all prayers, praises, readings, bible study time for those few minutes in the morning. I'd leave the house on a full spiritual tank of gas but no refueling prayer breaks until the next day. If I ate the way I pray sometimes, I'd be malnourished. For optimal health and sustained energy, I need to take in regular spiritual nourishment and communicate with God more than once a day.

Other than dinner, I eat many meals and snacks solo. That day I invited God to be my breakfast, lunch, and snack date. Each time I sat down to eat I wrote my needs and gratitude list which centered my thinking. Writing while eating slowed my consumption rate because I'd take a bite, write what was on my heart, take another bite, and repeat. This ritual became like a continuous drip to my soul. Each day is filled with virtual sugar and salt experiences and the steady diet of prayer manna decreases spikes and drops in sugar and salt levels.

This consistent spiritual nourishment gives me a more realistic summary of the day. Instead of saying the day is great or otherwise, my prayer log captures both sides of the day's story. Reviewing entries indicate how much "pre-worry" happened prior to this habit of eating and writing together.
Prayer logging also pinpointed how often I focused on one upsetting hour and overlooked twenty three other hours. Instead of allowing myself to mindlessly spin bald tires, I write my concerns throughout the day and (do my best to) trust God's perpetual traction to avoid a spiritual blow-out. As

the Bible instructs: "Pray without ceasing" (1 Thes. 5:17 NIV).

Our Pastor affirms frequent connections with God when he appealed to the church to take a "Fifteen minute chair challenge." He invited us to be God hogs on the couch potato scene. Pastor Chris encouraged us to find a chair near a place that represents sitting at the feet of Jesus. Find a scripture or chapter from the bible and spend fifteen minutes every day asking Him what to take away from that reading. The small intentional use of time reaps nearly two hours by the end of the week and enormous returns on investment.

I read an article about a lady reaching out to one person every day. She saw many lonely or empty people and knew she couldn't connect with everyone, but she could connect with someone. Each morning, this lady asked "who and how can I elevate someone today?" She took "bite size chunks" toward a larger goal that reaped a buffet of impact for many people. Her story inspired me to insert a touch of joy into at least one person every day. I wrote names of people who could use an extra surprise to display their smile.

This present may be a handwritten note, favorite candy, phone call, greeting card for no specific holiday. The gift could include a meal, an anonymously given coffee shop gift card, a block of time to babysit. 365 days each year to treat others to unexpected gifts offers me contagious energy that stems from watering someone else's spirit.

During my first year of "Tinker Bell" ministry, I pledged to add value to 365 *different* people or causes. There are days when I have more time to give. There are times when I have more money, or seasons when I have more creative energy to offer others. In the resource pool, I always have at least one asset of time, money, creativity, or energy. As long as I have breath, I have *something* to add to a life beyond my own. I love when God uses me on His payroll to tend to a person or situation that organically crosses my path. I'm learning that when I adjust to a "Now Here" mindset instead of "Nowhere" attitude, I experience a pleasant shift. Stalling in my comfort zone leads me to No Where. Proactive motion advances me toward, "Now Here"! Same letters, alternative perspective.

SEASONAL COLLISION

I think there are certain times of the year when my actions are more in sync with the way my body is designed. As a person who requires a lot of light, I notice how much more willing I am to run during spring and summer. Outdoor light, no matter how intense, beckons me toward activity, defaulting to overall optimism.

During Thanksgiving and Christmas one year, I received enlightenment from a friend who shares my need for much daylight. We were talking about holiday traditions and anticipated time off from work. I confessed being unmotivated to face shopping crowds and filter through noise. She chimed in that she most wanted a soft blanket and an evening alone with a book and mug of hot chocolate. I wanted to hire someone to wrap presents and decorate. She approached her family's gift exchange with project manager logic: "Why would I stand in Target with my $20 wondering what to buy Suzy Q, while she's standing just a few aisles down with her $20 wondering what to buy me? Why not stop the insanity and use the $20 for what we need most?" She and I laughed and steered the conversation toward Thanksgiving and Christmas outreaches. We listed our favorite seasonal delights including peppermint bark, Christmas shows, the smell of pine, pumpkin anything, happy faced reindeer, Angel Tree gifts, and warm sweaters.

I'm not a Scrooge. I have a generous spirit. Why then has it become my uphill climb to greet the holiday season with wonder? I embrace gratefulness being a key to deep rooted joy. Our family focuses on Jesus' birth. There's a magical sense when jingle bells or a Christmas song introduce a commercial. I empathize with people who have suffered loss and the holiday season can add weighted anxiety. I understand some people's pressure to create memorable gatherings. There are people who cannot financially provide a holiday meal, much less gifts. I'm blessed to have my needs covered so why do I foster such a sour outlook in November and December?

As I continued mulling over my source of holiday heaviness, I concluded that the American calendar year of large events collides with a body's natural rhythms. Bears, groundhogs, skunks, bees, and other animals use winter months for hibernating. They use dark cooler weather to hunker down and sleep deeply. If animals are awakened during hibernation, they become agitated, not unlike yanking a teenager out of bed before 10:00 a.m.

With hibernation for creatures coinciding with climate and daylight patterns, I relate my daylight savings' behavior to animal instincts: grouchy as a bear; casting an attitudinal 5:00 groundhog shadow; smelly as a skunk when I venture outside past dark; sting like a bee because I get painfully cold easily. The year's peak holidays arrive when the only thing I want to wrap is my body under a blanket. I'm grab flannel sheets from our bedroom closet while the material world is grabs holiday deals from store shelves. I look outside for the wintery moon's brushed glow, but neon Christmas lights flash instead. Silent night seems mocked in comparison to the ho-ho-ho's and amplified electronic gadgets in surround sound. The mall traffic drivers seem like the greatest flurry of flakes.

During the time when my body is designed to operate in lower gear, the marketing world thrusts me into four-wheel drive. This collision between a physical season and the perceived expectations of the Christmas season invites an element of chaos. Just as each person is affected differently when awakened, the holidays affect people in disparate ways. Not all animals hibernate, so the squirrels, elk, birds, and rabbits of the world, may be less affected by blizzards of holiday activity. For those who trek like groundhogs and bees during winter, the season of lights can be emotionally dark.

In many Christian churches, Advent begins a time to intentionally prepare our hearts for the birth of Christ. It's a time designated to reflect, to recreate the anticipation of Jesus' birth. The Advent season continues as we eagerly await Jesus' return to restore this broken world.

Our pastor preached a seasonal message from Luke 2's account of the Christmas story. He asked us to determine which story character we related to most. He offered how the innkeeper's response to

Mary and Joseph's plea may be equivalent to December's busyness. When we don't make time to acknowledge Jesus' birth, or that Mary was even pregnant while Joseph stressed to find a place for Mary's labor and delivery, it's like saying, "there's no room at the inn."

I pictured a knock on the door of my heart's inn. Do I make room to fully welcome Jesus, especially to host Him for His birthday party? Into which rooms do I invite Jesus? Is He front and center in the living room, or do I limit Him to a spare closet where I mingle with Him between entertaining other guests? Do I meet Him in the garage for an alignment when His party isn't tuned-up to my expectations? Maybe He can do a quick wash up in the guest bathroom. Are there parts of my "inn" where Jesus is off limits?

Between Thanksgiving and Christmas, I'm tempted to do a reaction check when someone asks if I'm ready for Christmas. Instead of a summarizing our Christmas preparations or gently share Christian holiday witness, I want to ask, "What does 'ready for Christmas' look like to *you*?" My intent isn't to create awkwardness, but hopefully gain understanding about people's values, traditions, and maybe a story about a seasonal memory.

Back to front and center. What spirit am I selling during the holidays? I want to give away an upbeat Christmas spirit. Not everyone will buy this gift but they could make good use of it when I freely give it like Christ did on Christmas morning. How can I step out of hibernation and tend to the human "sparrows"? I want to be someone who helps restore holiday joy. To light from the inside no matter how dark it is outside!

VERBAL CHICKENPOX

Our church small group did a study about words we say and words we hear. Our leader gave us a weekly challenge to listen to comments that people spoke on the radio. We were invited to write conversation topics or sentences that DJ's, commercials, or callers used and share them with the group the following week.

It was a wake-up call to hear our group's compiled list. Frequently used phrases included, "I just about died," or "this is going to kill me." To our knowledge, none of the people who spoke about situations nearly killing them left earth or ended up in the hospital that day. "I'm so tired" or I'm sick" were also recurring comments. Some radio shows invited call-ins from parents. A few moms and dads said, "My kid is going to drive me to drink," and "My daughter is driving me crazy" (I secretly wondered why kids were driving the household instead of parents taking the wheel).

Using the week of word observations, our group discussed the value and power of words. We agreed that when someone said they were tired or sick, they seemed to act upon that label all day, or consecutive days. One man said he went to work feeling completely rested and healthy one morning, but his demeanor changed after simply hearing a co-worker's sleepy diagnosis. He said the person's dreary lamentation left him worn-out, despite his upbeat arrival to work one hour prior to the droopy discourse.

A man from our group who blatantly addresses melodramatic talk as literal interpretation shared an example of his employee assigned to an atypical project. The employee's reaction to the new task was a sigh and statement, "This is going to kill me." Our group member responded, "I asked (employee name) that in the unlikely event of death stemming from this project, I'd appreciate a refrain from bloodshed on company desks." This same group member recapped one of his gym experiences. He said there was a sweaty person on the treadmill next to him who exclaimed, "I'm going to die." Our group member answered, "You're exactly right. One day you will die, just like the rest of us."

We initially laughed at his frank approach, but later talked about how his comebacks to spontaneous remarks invited us to pause before speaking. The leader used Matthew 12:36-37 as that evening's foundation. "But I tell you that everyone will have to give account on the day of judgment for every empty word they have spoken. For by your words you will be acquitted, and by your words you will be condemned" (NIV).

This discussion taught us about the magnitude of our words. We shared examples about how we speak lightness and heaviness into existence. Some of our perceptions stem from fear and we create false prophecies. We talked about using one past experience to sometimes determine all future responses, even when a new situation involves different people or different conditions. One lady said she has a habit of bringing yesterday's clouds over today's sunshine.

Our group leader said she believes there are far more premature deaths and mental health issues based on the impact of words. She asked us to count how many times we hear or have heard, "She's nuts", "That drives me crazy," "This is insane." The enemy doesn't decipher between sarcasm and literal interpretation. Satan will use any wise crack or flippant words as food for thought to use as ammo for attack.

Tig and I met with that small group two years after that teaching and it continues to sway my choice toward speaking or not speaking certain words. I used to fill any conversation space with my opinion or observations that I defined as humorous. Later on, I realized that my classification of funny sometimes held a sting and other people have a desire to weigh in with their ideas. I view people as more attractive when they choose to inspire rather than impress the listener. I discovered the flame of judgment would be extinguished if I didn't fan the conversational fire with my outpouring of hot air.

I'm frequently reminded about the wisdom from *Bambi's* bunny Thumper. As a baby, Thumper's mom taught him, "If you can't say something' nice, don't say nothin' at all." I wrote that sentence with

Thumper's cartoon voice playing in my head, leading me down a rabbit trail other gems of wisdom from animated movies. Those lessons can be saved for another chapter...

Bridling my tongue still requires heightened security alert. I've made progress toward verbal temperance, but caution myself against being short-fused when someone groans, "Is this day *ever* going to end?" Or when I chew my lip to bite back a retort after cheerfully asking someone how they're doing and they respond "Could be worse." Reverting to lessons from cartoon characters, I think of Eeyore from Winnie the Pooh. Eeyore consistently spews verbal chickenpox. Winnie the Pooh shows greater stamina than I do to endure Eeyores in my path. Instead of using compassion for Miss-Frequent-Flier-on-the-Downtrodden-Runway, I picture her negative words as chickenpox.

Without immunization, chickenpox becomes contagious. Without a word filter, words can be those uncomfortable, scratchy, and spreading pox. Before the awareness of word power, I routinely made chickenpox comments. Now those comments make me feel like I have a feverish rash under my skin. Those barbs can cause scars if mentally picked apart and scratched. It appears that some people are more immune to wordy chickenpox, though I believe downtrodden vocabulary seeps into our mental digestive tract to cause unpleasant side effects.

To lessen the spreading of verbal chickenpox, I'm learning to bite my tongue more often. (Sometimes I need to bite my entire face). It's my Iron Mouth Marathon, one step of striding and strengthening at a time.

REQUIRED HEALTH CARE

Tig was promoted to a managerial role to lead and coach a team of 13 employees. He discovered absenteeism to be his heaviest burden. He recognizes employees occasionally get sick or miss work due to doctor appointments. I'm maturing toward elevated compassion like Tig possesses. I respond to chronic illness from the same people in a much different way (different *sounds* more gracious).

My umbrella for best health is taking a daily multi-vitamin and eating mostly whole foods. I'd be interested in having a statistician conduct a study to track employee attendance based on people who regularly take a multi-vitamin and people who do not. I'm not suggesting that a daily multi-vitamin is a solution to perfect job attendance, but I'd be curious to compare a study's results.

I picture this health care scenario as envisioned only from the scope of Christina Eder: a vitamin dispenser would be near the employee entrance or time clock. Each day before workers began their shift, a human resource employee or nurse would hand employees a multi-vitamin, a cup of water, and a simple light carb/protein meal. This healthy start procedure could fall under a company nutritional health insurance policy, and possibly offer company discount.

I'd also like to see a link between vitamins, nutrition, and absenteeism study tracking medical costs before and after this healthier start scenario. Categories could include employees feeling better overall, less absenteeism, fewer doctor visits, more energy at and away from work, weight loss, greater focus, less tension. Initially, this vitamin, water, nourishing meal approach may be met with resistance. Flex time, car allowances, paid breaks, meal reimbursements, and clothing expense accounts sometimes faced opposition when those were introduced.

As an unsolicited spokesperson for Flintstones chew tabs, I remember Mom reminding me that a daily multi-vitamin was essential. She used to place the colorful Barney, Fred, or Dino vitamin in a plastic cup as part next to my toothbrush. I thought the habit was just something Moms taught their kids to keep Wilma and Betty on the vitamin character payroll.

After the dinosaur days, I graduated to more adult-like vitamins, and when I got to college vitamins became a commodity that didn't fit my oatmeal/egg budget. It was during a yearly physical when I told my doctor about waning energy, more colds, and less concentrated thoughts. His first question, "Do you take a multi-vitamin?" My answer was no and he prescribed a multi-vitamin regime for 30 days with a follow-up evaluation. I appreciated sustained energy, less mood swings, improved cognitive function, and decreased recovery time in case of illness. I continue the multi-vitamin habit that my Mom taught.

As a less wise person, I mistakenly dismissed Mom's advice as something written on her tablets from bedrock days. Even though Fred Flintstone is a man from my past, my adult multi-vitamin fills nutritional gaps that my diet "may" not provide. I propose a world policy to take a multi-vitamin daily. We could all reap the health benefits, especially the makers of multi-vitamins!

DRYCLEANED ARMOR

Often, my prayers get answered in visual aid form. God uses routine tasks or situations to provide clarity or new perception from a seemingly ordinary circumstance.

Our pastor taught about putting on our full spiritual armor every day. He talked about dressing our self with protection similar to a knight preparing for battle. Like a shower, armoring up cannot be carried over from yesterday and it cannot be done for tomorrow.

This armor (Eph. 6:14-17) instructs Christians to stand firm with the belt of truth buckled around our waists. We are to hold that breastplate of righteousness in place, ready to shield ourselves from fiery arrows (hopefully not literal ones!). Our feet are fitted with readiness and peace as we hike virtual mountains and tread amidst slippery valleys. The armor closet includes a shield of faith, a helmet of salvation, and a sword of the Spirit to activate the word of God. I frequently borrow a tongue bridle from James 3's armor closet!

In visualize an armored solider, I have a cross bow of thoughts. Paul wrote his message to the Ephesians and was speaking figuratively. He encouraged all believers to spiritually armor themselves in the same way a soldier protects himself when he advances to the front line. I picture myself plodding along a running path in a full-blown knight suit going about my day pretending to be Joan of Arc.

Pulling a 6:30 mile in metal get-up presents comical imagery, but in my mind's eye, I notice a spirit of boldness in dressing for battle. I shared this visual with a co-worker and we began using a code of armor in the office when we faced hardships. When someone or something tested our patience, the one not engaged in that particular battle silently prayed armor over the other. If negative dynamics intensified, we'd say "helmet or belt" just loud enough for the other person's reassurance. That armor code drew our sword to fight with a more Christ-like manner. After heated attacks subsided, we'd jokingly say, "Whoo! I have to readjust my breastplate after *that* one!" or "I need to tighten up the chin strap on my helmet!"

Literally speaking, laundering armor could be more daunting than washing every day clothes. I have yet to see a washing machine with a chain mail or metal setting. After a day on the earthly battlefield, I picture myself taking off that cumbersome suit and laying it at Jesus' feet. Overnight, He takes extra care to dry clean and polish my armor so it's ready for the next day. He can reattach buckles, tighten chinks in the metal shell, sharpen my sword, and place it by the side of my bed. His Word is my receipt that the protective sealant and cleaning are finished, ready to be picked up as soon as I get out of bed the next day.

Some nights after a metaphorically bloody battle behind enemy lines, I wonder how God will remove tough stains, patch holes, or make the armor shine in time for the next day's combat. Each morning, I wake to see a flawless new suit in my armor closet, waiting to be fully used. Onward Christian soldier, the revelry horn is blowing!

911 PRAYERS

While this is fresh and raw, I'm going to write something that occurred to me during quiet time. Lately, I've lit two candles on the shelf beside where I take morning solitude. When distracting thoughts about the day's events or random thoughts scamper across my mind, I make an effort to laser point my attention on those two candles. This morning, I was exceptionally restless and agitated for no particular reason. I didn't have a foreboding sense that anything was off kilter or I needed to do something specific, but I was unusually fidgety.

I wrestled to find peace despite what felt like a swarm of bats colliding with each other. In this jumping bean status, I tried reading my Bible out loud, writing a letter to God, and repeating scripture verses. No amount of devotional manna was calming my spirit and I was growing more impatient by the minute.

Finally, I turned on the radio to K-Love (K-Love is not a paid book sponsor, but they are #1 on my radio pre-sets). The song by Casting Crowns, "Just Be Held" was playing. The singer proclaims: "When you're on your knees and answers seem so far away. You're not alone, stop holding on, and just be held." Bingo! That aha sensation resembled running in shoes too tightly laced and finally stopping to loosen them instead of pounding the pavement on nearly numb feet.

I let the song play out and questioned how often I frantically place a 911 call to God and expect Him to answer faster than a running cockroach when the lights are turned on. I recognize that God can *instantly* move on my request. Why do I not only *make* a request, but then dictate how *fast* I think God needs to answer it in the way *I* want Him to. That awareness was like a healthy serving of insubordinate toast for breakfast!

I thought about how my desperation cry prayers are like a 911 call. When I call, I expect emergency workers to be dispatched. Even if the time seems to pass slowly or the workers aren't tending to my emergency immediately, I trust that help *is* on the way. I wait it out, trying to claim peace and comfort while waiting. An ambulance or fire truck cannot arrive sooner if I repeatedly dialed 911. I take into consideration that a police officer may be slightly delayed because he's working another emergency. Siren sounds indicate that help is on the way, but heavy traffic may slow their arrival. I have a level of assurance that my 911 call *is* being attended.

With this newfound perspective, I realize I must develop more trust in God's faithfulness. Even when I'm unfaithful and wavering, He is faithful and steady. He spoke the world into existence, He rose on Easter morning after dying three days prior, and cares for the sparrows. How can I have more trust in humans when they assure me that help is on the way but I don't exude confidence in my Protector and

Shepherd? I'm learning to grasp and embrace His gift to "just be held."

If you have not heard the Casting Crowns song, *Just Be Held*, I encourage you to listen to this touch from heaven. I share these two significant uplifts on my journey toward Eternal Life, the time when I get to meet the "Original 911 Dispatcher" face to face!

STEPPING OUT

As I write this section, I recently left a job I had for a decade. During those ten years, my salary increased, the company funded part of my higher education degree, benefits were tremendous, and the location was close to home. Work hours were better than banker hours and job duties varied widely. Co-workers were partly-to-mostly sunny with occasional storms. I re-read the opening lines to this chapter. I have gone two weeks without a paycheck but have immense peace about moving toward a new career season.

For the past couple of years, there was an underlying heaviness in my spirit when I went to work. Not every day and not all day long. Being a firm believer and faithful participant in holistic health, I first took inventory of my nutrition to trace the source of funk. I wanted to make sure I wasn't eating excessive carbs, missing protein, not consuming enough water, lacking in vitamins, or being deficient in minerals. I found some nutritional tweaks and tightened small gaps that could be leaking this non-situational sadness into my spirit.

With nutritional reins tightened, my overall physical health benefitted, but there was still an encroaching sense of blue. Being raised in a 'toughen up', 'there are people worse off than you' environment, I feared that somehow I had grown self-absorbed. My lifestyle indicated church involvement and some social outings. Group settings are never my default, but I was regularly surrounding myself with people. I make a point of smiling and enthusiastically greeting others. Since fifth grade, I have kept a gratitude journal and diary. (To secure my most valuable eleven year old thoughts, I used babysitting money to buy a diary with a puny gold key on an equally puny beaded chain to safeguard against snoops). In my quest for renewed happiness, I grabbed my recent journals to scan for gratitude entries. I was thankful for recorded uplifts, yet that "something is missing" theme kept popping up.

For weeks, I was generally out of sorts, but avoided the unsettling distraction, intentionally maintaining a business-as-usual routine. It's been proven that buried feelings and unaddressed items resurface somewhere, sometime, some place. Fast forward to avoid adding another long testimony that has already been written, studied, discussed or learned from. The bottom line: my story mirrors the frequently discussed "something's missing in my life so I need to find it and figure it out before I can move forward." I have a different body, different circumstances, different way of trouble shooting, different background than another reader has, yet the crux remains: What is my purpose and what in the heck should I do in this restless valley? In prayer, "Lord, help me simply wait for "it" to unfold and not unravel during Your process!"

With internally gnawing scab intact, I began forming a virtual callus over my heart as I noticed this mental pit deepening. My yearly physical showed great blood panel results, I had no signs of depression, got restful sleep, solid nutrition, social outings, sunshine, vitamins, climbing a mountain on my lunch hour wearing red flip flops and a purple hat, oops! The climbing was an exaggeration. This uphill trek was more like shimmying a shared glass wall. I was showing signs of edginess despite following every Joe Schmoe's version of *3011 Ways to Trumpet your Calling Without Cutting Off your Horns* (rhinos, unicorns, and trumpet players take no offense!)

The calendar narrowed in on my one-year work contract. I faced the renewal decision with a mustered up spirit, "OK, fresh year! You can do this! Let's get fired up!" Translate: "So basically Christina, continue to stuff your emotions, put on a new contract mask, hide your unattended callus from last year and keep going." Sadly, my 'go get 'em slugger' facade grew more noise sensitive. I had no patience whatsoever for what I deemed idle chit chat. Internally, I was shouting, "Who cares about your weekend, just get to work!" I worked at a school where I often said I'd adopt almost every one of those 600 students if I had a large enough house. I was honest then. Now, I struggled to tell any of them good morning. It physically hurts to admit that ugliness, especially because hypocrisy is a hot button I sidestep at all costs.

One day after school, a couple of students I'd ordinarily vote as "most likely knights to get a dragon out of a funk" walked toward my office. Usually I would have been humbled that they stayed after school to share their news. Instead of waiting in my office to hear (what I later learned from a co-worker) their incredibly life changing update, I did a quick about face. I hurriedly acted like I needed copies at the printer down the hall. I laughed off my office escape by justifying, "That's another terrific reason for running so I can be in shape to make quick getaways like that." I rationalized my interpersonal avoidance thinking my absence would open doors for other staff members to invest in students' lives.

When I got back to my desk, our receptionist said how those students' faces fell and shoulders slumped when she told them I left to 'make copies'. She added that they knew I usually wasn't away from my desk very long so they lingered in the lobby because they wanted me to be the first person to hear their news. Thud! In hearing this, I wanted to make another escape. Not running from others this time, but running from myself.

Somehow I had gone from "a ray of sunshine" to a thick haze of heavy humid air. I finally opened up to a trusted co-worker. I needed a straight forward, no coddling perspective from someone who would fully listen. I desperately sought someone who wouldn't interrupt the unleashing of my beasty feelings with their topper story slightly resembling my rabid dog thought narrative.

I prefaced my plea to my coworker, "Please hear me out and temporarily suspend your judgment or advice." I told him how I informed our principal ten years ago that I would retire from that school. At the time, I stated that with authenticity. I recapped how summers used to be difficult because I preferred to do the paperwork and office tasks with kids in the mix. I laughed when the principal advised me that if I ever got to a point when I *didn't* feel that excitement, it was time to cash it in. I assured him this wouldn't be the case and added how I'd be the first in line to vote for year-round school.

This confession was dumped on the co-worker's ears and I was ready for his input. We agreed about significant adjustments in education over the past ten years. We expect staff changes, innovative programs, and alternative equipment to handle our jobs. We understand career focus ebbs and flows, the natural cycle in any life. Had I not adapted? Where did my attitude shift? Why did my anticipation wane for students to stop and simply say hi, with no office need? I wasn't ready to dissect the downward spiral process. I wanted some imaginative career stimulant to reload energy that used to be a natural shot in the arm!

I had just placed my pancreas on the chopping block, verbally addressing this gorge I had fallen into. This co-worker, also a friend, unknowingly dissected this pancreatic lump with one question. "Have you ever thought of taking a silent retreat?"

Thinking he humorously suggested a silent retreat to get me to come up for air, I laughed and said, "A silent retreat would be one way to get me quiet!" When I realized he wasn't joking, I listened to a solution that became one of life's defining moments. Christopher's suggestion led me to a silent retreat that knocked on calloused doors of my heart, allowed a cleansing bleed-out, and invited healing to begin. For the rest of the school year, I dedicated many running miles to consider retreat options and wrestle with whatever had stolen my joy.

Fast forward from November's silent retreat brainstorm until June's flood of revelation.

What exactly is a silent retreat? Each person defines a silent retreat differently. I believe every person holds a bounty of reactions. There are varied levels of openness involved with self-inventory of deeper understanding.

I naturally thrive in low levels of stimuli. Our home has minimal amounts of furniture and our walls are free of décor. We don't play music as background noise, we don't have a TV, we close doors gently, and our ring tones are set on the lowest volume setting.

The external noise is intentionally low, however sometimes my head chatter speaks with surround sound volumes. It hasn't learned the art of using its "inside voice." I personalized this silent retreat to quiet and calm my swirl of thoughts twice a day for one to three hour blocks. My goal was to think at a slower linear pace. I wanted my mind to resemble a soft glowing campfire instead of a grand finale firework display. To do this, I chose the word gentle. Gentle became my one word centerpiece to display when my thought table hollered, "All you can eat buffet!" Even though I didn't know what segments B through Y looked like on my retreat journey, I knew point A and wanted Z to end with tamed clarity.

Our school office summer schedule was abbreviated to 9:00-2:00 hours with Fridays off. The shortened work hours would have allowed ample silence and search for clarity. However, our house had been on the market for months and was set to close at the end of June. Prior to the house offer, I was smack dab in the final decision process of choosing a retreat center experience. We were relieved that the house finally sold, but the summer would be used to pack, move, unpack, and transition into our new home. Two weeks before closing, our HVAC system went out during the buyer's final walk through. Ryan, a friend of ours, owns a heating and cooling company but he was on vacation and unable to check out what we considered an emergency.

Cliff note summary for an extensive horror story: Ryan got back from vacation, answered our HVAC service call before his other customers, but said he'd have to replace the entire unit instead of repairing it. Despite being in the midst of his busiest season, he promised to complete the job prior to house closing.

We planned to congratulate the new home owners with a restaurant gift card. Instead, we rolled out the red carpet for them and purchased a new $6000 HVAC system with a 10 year warranty. Tig and I joke (years later) how we raised the bar for typical housewarming (in this case, house cooling) gifts. "Go big or go home" opened doors to a different view of that saying. Now when we get Housewarming invitations, we'll call fellow party attendees to make sure they haven't already purchased an HVAC system for the new home owners. We'd be uncomfortable arriving at a housewarming party with a large appliance, only to find out someone duplicated our gift idea.

We closed on the house. We moved. We were $6000 lighter. Thanks to involuntarily pulling a generosity card out of our wallet, my silent retreat decision became simple. It would move to the back burner since we were served a large stew pot of not-so-heartwarming events. With the unexpected expenses, moving transitions, and my growing weariness, I wasn't incorporating much divine silence about anything.

A few days after the house closing, I sat in our new apartment sunroom and felt a nudge about the silent retreat. Throughout the day, that pull grew more persistent and the continual desire toward a silent retreat morphed. The urgency became like an insistent three year old tapping me on the shoulder with repeat play, "Mom, Mom, look at this!" I can only half-heartedly listen so long before that toddler knows he's being put off. The shoulder tapping graduated to an arm tug followed by a louder voice, "Mom! Are you listening? Can you *hear* me Mom? Maaaaaaaawm"! I needed to address this persistent appeal.

Was I *really* to take a silent retreat despite logistics and finances, or was this my own nagging because I had my heart set on this experience? I grabbed my prayer journal and wrote God a rush order for His clarity. Within minutes, He delivered His answer. I was to take a silent retreat at home. At *home*? What about the trickling brook behind the quaint cottage pictured in my retreat lodge ad? Our new apartment was pleasant, but it didn't include sweet aromas wafting from the kitchen as someone else cooked meals. What about the spiritual director who would guide me through the unscheduled restlessness? What about the nature trails behind the cabin? We just moved to a congested area of town. Car horns were a far cry from geese honking. At home, tweets would much more likely be technologically generated instead of chirping birds in resort trees.

God graciously waited for me to finish my mini rant and then shed light on how we'd create a silent retreat experience together. With the recent rapid $6000 weight loss from our bank account, coupled with vacation time used to move, I didn't have paid hours left. God provided a solution for that objection too. He was extremely clear about incorporating my 9:00-2:00 summer work hours into a stay at home silent retreat.

The first silent session was from 7-8:30 a.m. to read daily devotionals, growth books, sit in silence, review journal entries, and write insights as they surfaced. The 2:30-3:30 after work session was to be for confession and cleansing my mind from less than virtuous behaviors. Because God was so straight forward, I gained a clearer vision for His retreat mission. All aboard! I was newly stoked for retreat week, gathered necessary supplies, and jumped in the next day ready to grow. The first morning session passed quickly and I headed to work finding myself anticipating more reading. I wanted to finish the flood of thoughts from that 90 minute block of time.

I jotted down topics I wanted to write about when I got home for the afternoon retreat segment. 2:30 came. Armed with paper and pen, I sat in our sunroom, ready to process thoughts from the day. I drew a blank in trying to recall what seemed so important to write. I was fidgety and unable to sit still more than four minutes. My body implored me to go running as was my afternoon routine. My determination to obey God's guidance won. There were new rules and my mind and body were not playing well with each other.

Ok. Re-establish stillness. Clear your mind. Pause to think. Another blank stare. A lame attempt to extract creative ideas. A second chance to cleanse my mind. Had I developed some sort of Teflon Brain Syndrome? Everything that had once stuck on my mind had suddenly released and slid off!

More sitting, more waiting, time was ticking. I grew more distracted with concern that I was wasting time instead of investing time. My mind started visiting everywhere beyond the apartment sunroom. I was edgy. This was not the peace, experience, or space I expected when I pictured a silent retreat! Looking up, I asked God to send some key to open the padlock of my brain waves. Instead of a key, He simply reminded me of the afternoon retreat's purpose. Confession and cleansing. (I always know when 'that voice' is really God because my "God voice" sounds like Dan Haggerty, the star who played Grizzly Adams on TV).

Confession and cleansing. My first confession is to you the reader. This is the place I took a writing hiatus because confession forced me to look at ugliness. The process was more painful, more unveiling, and more intense than I expected. I grappled with the thought that reading through the cleansing phase of my mind would be tedious. I would have rather skipped to the happy roses section that follows the thorns. I figured (read: I lied to myself) that if I ignored the cleansing and confession pieces of my retreat, I could magically make those raw, peel-the-skin-back letters of purification disappear. I couldn't be judged if I omitted certain details. God reminded of my written declaration from the beginning of this book that this was a transparent collection of running mile thoughts. More complete pictures are woven by knitting many mental strands of yarn together. So with a deep breath and plunging forward with full life over still life honesty, here I go…

Back to the afternoon conundrum between running and sitting still…God made it evident that I was to sit with paper and pen to write about situations, people, memories that were heavy on my mind. The criterion He gave me was to write as fast as I could, not paying attention to grammar, not writing for any audience, to picture myself as if I was pulling out all dirty water from a deep well. To invite the highest level of purification, I immediately shred the paper deluges when I finished written purges. No proof reading, no analyzing, no attempting to answer questions. Simply write. I used those shredded paper stripes as an offering to God, asking Him to compost old thoughts and transform them into something more life-giving.

I wrote about recent irritants and weaknesses. I scrawled everything: from avoiding an acquaintance because I wasn't wearing my social hat that day to my annoyance with the sound of a co-worker's fingernail clipping. The more situations and emotions that surfaced, the more I faced my depths of mental pollution. The 2:30 hour passed, I shred the confessions and walked to the dumpster to dispose them. On my way to the garbage bin, I wondered why I spent vast amounts of time clogging my thoughts with toxic chemicals. Why waste head space on floods of dirty water when I could have clearer waterways of thinking? Since I was philosophizing about silent retreat meditations, I might as well reflect on my reasons for shaving with dull razors. What makes me continue to buy single use, half-a-blade shavers, especially for the summer? Why do I write with cheap pens that either skip or dent the paper? And just when *will* I finally purchase new underwear instead of settling for saggy baggy drawers? There's more to life than mentally swatting gnats!

The next morning instead of using the 7:00-8:30 session for quiet time, reading, and journaling, I was tempted to write more irritants I missed from yesterday's recall. I figured if I freed my innards from all mental toxins, I'd speed up the purifying process. I got out of my silent study mode" to grab scrap paper when I remembered the purpose of the morning retreat was to ask God to clarify and teach while I listened and learned. Cleansing and confession was for the afternoon. Both sessions held two distinct purposes and I was determined to align with God's direction. I dug deep for discipline and went back to my silent time out, saving the paper for afternoon refinement.

This wrestling/dance routine between God and me continued for a full week. Mornings to read, afternoon to write. Each day God gave me desires, concepts to think about, a perpetual invitation to allow creativity to replace mental traps I had fallen (or stepped) into. A fresh supply of life was dripping back into my veins.

I planned on a one week retreat, using Friday to reflect, and recap the experience with Christopher when we returned to school in August. Friday arrived, I finished my confession letter at 3:30 and was ready to mark off my virtual retreat goal. Take a silent retreat. Check box. Next goal.

With a sense of accomplishment, I made dinner without really giving much thought to thanking God for the incredible ways He showed up and invested Himself in me that week. I was standing by the stove when wham! An unsettling sadness catapulted me. Wait! The week of retreating was over, I grew stronger through clarity and now an emotional cannon ball blasted my heart? Why? What is going on? Shouldn't peaceful bliss from a silent retreat last longer than a runner's six minute mile pace?

I wanted to quickly expel the unwelcomed pang of rekindled sadness. I paused the dinner making scene to check my mental frying pan for burnt edges. Why had God gone out to dinner and left me with dirty dishes?! After the dust of my prideful assumption cleared, I realized I was the one who left the retreat to make dinner. I didn't pause long enough to ask God what He wanted next from me. He *wanted* me to seek His comfort, His providence, His wisdom, His strength. It's humbling to know He has every quality, unlimited resources, and He *wants* to share it with His kids? That's a concept I still struggle to wrap my head around.

I internally clutched, shifted, and put my thinking in full-throttle reverse. The back-up beeper sounded. As I mentally moved from the driver's seat to the passenger seat, I asked God how *He* wanted me to use this week's newfound lessons. With a sense of conviction, not condemnation, I waited for His answer. I waited some more. Still waiting. "Here I am Lord, just patiently waiting for your answer. Yup, still waiting. Just you and me God. All here, ready to listen. Did I mention, I'm fully here, ready to hear from You? I really mean it this time. I'm letting you drive." Was His lack of response my payback for not checking with Him in the first place? Had God made a spontaneous decision to take a silent retreat too? Critical note: I know this is *not* the way God operates, but at that moment, I stepped into the poopy diaper stage of my Christian walk.

I didn't want to pull another insubordination move by leaving the question on the table before God spoke. I spent that evening walking with Tig, straightening the house, and brushing our dogs with the underlying watchfulness that God would answer my prayer soon. Even though the earlier wave of sadness had subsided, I felt unsettled. I hoped that with all the closeness I had built with God in one week, I somehow moved up His answered prayer answered list. The toddler in the messed up diaper returned in my head and I wanted His answer *now*.

As the weekend unfolded, I released my fixation about hearing God's answer immediately. Certainly if He wanted me to do something with the silent retreat lessons, He'd give me assignments. Monday morning rolled around and from just one week, I grew to anticipate the silent retreat routine. My morning run was followed by 1 ½ hours of developing attentiveness. I was surprised at how quickly the 7:00-8:30 time frame passed. I craved to learn more from a wider span of development books and to examine the Word instead of skimming it. I revived to the point where God could have extended my life by 200 years and I wouldn't have enough time to explore a freshly opened world. I was equally amazed at how much I had discovered from just being quiet. The "white angel on my shoulder" side was shining. That's the picture I wanted to perpetually show.

After a weekend of waiting for God to coach me toward a detailed game plan, I had implication that I was to extend the silent retreat pattern for July. The sound of screeching brakes entered my head as I tried picturing God's response to my knee-jerk reaction. Just three days ago, I was telling God I was ready to do His will, whatever that may be. Now with the thought of more confession, I was back to wearing pull-ups for spiritually immature kids.

Deep down, I knew my resistance to more silence was out of fear. There could be lurking monsters I buried in recesses of my inner crawl space and God was inviting me to let Him shine light on them. In not grasping His unconditional love, understanding, and forgiveness, I worried God would uncover something that deemed me unworthy or He'd take away future blessings. I placed God in the human category and was convinced He'd be surprised by what may come out during this extended silent retreat. He graciously waited for me to come out of hiding and then invited me to leave my storage shed of lies.

I stopped wrestling, thanked Him for His answer, and recommitted to discovering the root of my prolonged sadness. I'd complete the in-home silent retreat for the month of July. In that morning's study time, I read about people who wrote forgiveness letters to relatives, boss, friend whom they felt had wronged them. Those testimonies held freedom and I wanted a piece of that released burden. I had no idea how excruciating it could be to draw past poison to the surface. I chose to write to a person I believed held the reins on my bondage cart of hurt. I knew I wasn't going to give my letter to the recipient. I doodled at the top of my paper in an effort to delay the impending pain and God reminded me He'd replace my dark with His light. I was burdened to inventory every dark place and ask God to replace a cold stony heart with a warm pliable model. I was getting a much better side of this deal, but I needed to do my part first.

I began writing the letter with a list of hurts coming to my mind immediately, followed by a burning lump in my throat as I fought against tears. I knew I needed to write through the pain but my stomach, head, hand, and pen were not cooperating. Between silence and willing myself to open up, the dam collapsed and I allowed myself to bleed out.

I feverishly penned hateful comments, situations, and conversations, until my tears resembled something more like rubber cement drainage. I used my sleeve to wipe my nose and face because if I stopped to get tissues, I was afraid I'd use the writing break as a barrier. There was still more toxic waste and I didn't want anything stopping me from fully emptying this septic tank of thoughts. It was 4:40 when I looked up at the clock with a shudder that felt like I had finally vomited all the mental and emotional poison I had ever carried. My writing finished with a dry heave conclusion, knowing there was nothing bitter left to release. I felt a bit woozy and my head was stiff from crying so hard, but least the tourniquet around my heart could be removed. It was time for honest healing to begin.

For the rest of July, I wrote one forgiveness letter each day. None of them were as taxing as the first letter, but still pivotal in the removal of unnecessary weight. I wrote about circumstantial hurt that didn't involve people but personal injury had manifested resulting from a chaos of events, timing, or misplaced words. I committed to write about any hairline fractures that threatened cracks or breaks in my foundation. Those written confession and cleansing afternoons were like a meat basting process. My heart was a piece of raw meat and God marinated His seasonings into my spirit. Sometimes He used enough 'conviction salt' so I felt the sting of my actions and then in one flawless swoop, He suctioned that salt from the wound before condemnation ruined life's flavor. I wanted to be soaked in sodium free water and be rid of all additives.

It was nearing the end of July and I felt more whole and more alive. Despite this euphoric enlightenment, I still hadn't identified reasons for lacking enthusiasm for the upcoming school year. I started writing a couple of questions-for-the-day at the top of my journal page, including money, parenting, and scheduling priorities. I left an entire page for: "Lord, what are Your goals for me this school year?" I left my journal open to that empty page to represent a clean slate. As I received direction, I wrote the answers. There were three primary focuses with several sub categories that school year:

1. Write a birthday card to every staff member with a sweet treat taped to the envelope. I would write a specific message about how their witness

added value to my life and then quietly put it in their mailbox on their birthday ("quietly" meaning, no personal fanfare, kudos to me for doing something nice).

2. Complete the 52 Virtues Project. A Google search for spiritual growth ideas led me to a life changing website called The 52 Virtues Project. For the next year, I would practice one virtue every week. I was to stick with only one, not jump ahead to an upcoming virtue or brush over ones in which I thought I had significant skill (aka "proudly mastered").

3. Pour into others, don't 'poor me'. Basically, crucify selfishness, widen my perspective lens and thoughtfully consider someone else's viewpoint.

Yes! Clarity! Yes! New vision! Yes! Answers with specifics! It's as if a trumpet sounded and an over-energized radio voice penetrates my clouded thoughts: *"Simply follow these three listed steps starting right now and your school year will have that renewed passion. You'll breathe fresh life into your career. But wait! There's more! Your introductory revelation kit will include sunglasses for a future so bright you'll have to wear shades; lip gloss as you pucker up your shine; and an extra large pair of big girl pants! Enjoy this overwhelming makeover all year. You'll feel as if you've eaten your Wheaties with a 3 Espresso chaser from morning until night!"*

Well, maybe the answer wasn't quite that intense, but Mr. Canned Radio's infomercial provided comic relief as I stepped forward to accept this year's mission. I swung into another pitch of "Go Big or Go Home" before hearing the "fine print guidelines"...

"And! If you order today, we'll also send you a First Aid Kit for the day when you step smack into the middle of your pride and realize that these three yearly goals are much simpler to read than to live! And that's not all! We'll include a tourniquet for when you've not only bitten your tongue but chewed through your entire lip in an effort to keep your mouth shut! Yes folks, we know you've been operating with high levels of honesty, so we're adding Dr. Candis B. Really-Happening's book, "101 Ways to Practice your Poker Face."

With the tremendous mental and spiritual conversion from a defining summer of my life, I wanted to show everyone how God had moved my world vision. Somehow, I thought my fire and enthusiasm could be infused into others. In addition to this year's career goals, I wanted to douse every situation in an encapsulating Kumbaya bubble.

I floated on that deceitful cloud and mistakenly bought a lying brand of pompous. I can truthfully say my motives were pure in believing that if I loved enough, prayed hard enough, encouraged enough, and listened hard enough, I could fix people's pains. I wanted to "make the world a better place" but had unknowingly developed what some call a savior complex. My grossly insubordinate self ran smack dab into the middle of pride rock (not from Disney's Lion King). I try to avoid running head first into anything, much less a quarry of self-righteousness. I claimed that yes, I was worthy. Yes, I was forgiven. Yes, God had worked in ways He never had before the silent retreat. Yes, it was life changing. But at no point of that defining summer did Jesus reach down, hand me His sandals, wink, nod His head and say, "Christina, you got this. It's Sabbath time for Me in Tennessee."

Learning to walk with Jesus reminds me of a life-sized Chutes and Ladders game. The game board has neatly lined rows of perfectly square blocks sequentially numbered from 1-100. When I land on a chute, I expect to be knocked down a few spaces. There's no collateral damage to my cardboard game piece and I continue climbing toward 100 on my next spin. In this teeter totter between chute and ladder, I continually ask God to show me how to boldly climb and when to be cautious while climbing near chutes. "Lord, how do I blend knowledge and experience with temperance? How can I be teaching without preaching?"

The month before I finished my school contract, my Dad offered navigational wisdom between life's chutes and ladders. Dad a human lighthouse fervently seeking God's every fiber in all facets of his life. He advises from accumulated wisdom he's gained from his nearly seventy revolutions around the sun.

I told Dad about my painful intersection of discernment between learning and lecturing. He knew about the outpour of God's teaching from my silent retreat. He also knew about the downpour of my overzealous evangelism from lack of discernment. We learned to bridge this gap of judgment by studying the following book together.

PARTING OF THE RED CREEK

Robert Morgan wrote *Rules of the Red Sea* and his book uncovered treasures beyond plankton from my mind. In this book Morgan explains how Moses and the Israelites found themselves caught between a devil and a deep (not so blue) sea. We too can become flooded by life's happenings, but even in seemingly hopeless situations God promises to create a way for us. I was so inspired by this written vessel that I asked my Dad to study *Rules of the Red Sea* together.

Dad lives thirteen hours from me so we scheduled phone dates for our book study. Each of the five Mondays in May 2015, we discussed two of the ten short lessons. When Dad and I set sail via telephone, neither of us predicted that in less than a month, we'd be confronting a personal Red Sea. Our family engaged those 10 rules of the Red Sea in July 2015 when Mom was diagnosed with a malignant brain tumor. Mom's cancer diagnosis resembled Pharoah's army quickly closing in on us while we walked on rocky terrain. Our family believes Mom lives eternally in the Promised Land. There will be perpetual waves of Mom's presence because she left many ripples of memories.

I intentionally leave the details of Mom's final seven weeks and one day on earth out of this book. Perhaps someday, more of our family's experiences may be written, but for now, there is no grammatical bridge between August 22, 2015 and today for many reasons.

It's been three years since Mom moved to heaven. Only now am I seeing the abundant treasure God shared by connecting Dad and me during our phone line classroom. Two people who learned from Robert Morgan's teaching *about* the Red Sea became the same people God chose as two of Mom's many caregivers *in* the Red Sea. Dad and I converted our phone inspirations to real life transformations.

I use the parting of the Red Sea to symbolically paint a broad portrait of our family landscape. I expect to pen new bridge designs that God will draw as I continue my journey toward the Promised Land. August 22, 2015 was Mom's pivotal Red Sea parting. Since then, I've experienced more Red Sea divisions, but also Red Creek and Red River movements.

The Red Creek and Red River movements are daily interactions. They represent smaller bodies of water, but are vital for steady flow of current. For example, I noticed a Red River opening while I delivered flowers during lunch hour traffic. That day, I'm almost certain all 368,000 people in our county were on the stretch of the road I was driving. I watched the minutes move faster than my vehicle and I asked for time redemption so I met the customer deadline. Within minutes of my holiest emergency prayer, "Please move this traffic or stop the clock

Lord", a space between cars opened, speed increased, and I got the tulip bouquet delivered to a smiling recipient. Additional bonus: The smiling recipient was the correct one, not a random person eager to take a bright spray of tulips from a floral delivery driver. Life and death didn't wage on this timely delivery, but in that moment, I equated the experience to parting a Red River.

Thankfulness didn't come as naturally for many months after Mom passing, but each time I purposely sought *anything* joyful, I claimed healing as a Red Creek trickle. In the torrents of Red Sea emotion, the remainder of 2015 felt like a large pointer finger stabbing me in the chest. Acute grief was like a distressing prod to keep me moving no matter where, no matter how. The gnawing was like running a marathon with large crowds cheering me forward but I was deaf to their encouragement. I was overcome by debilitating leg cramps, willing my feet to step. Labored breathing of grief clogged my chest, side stitches crippled me from crying so hard. I was overcome by one pointer finger poking cannons at my heart that I lost touch of nine other functioning fingers on the hands I was dealt. I just wanted to cross the finish line of grief, but wondered if there were rest stations along the way or if there would ever be a finish line to excruciating soul pain.

In January 26, 2016's journal entry I asked God to help me focus on His hand and outstretched arms instead of the enemy's taunting fingernails clawing my skin. I had people who served as co-pilots while I navigated my grief boat without Mom's earthly anchor. People sent cards of support long after the initial shock subsided. I had fully stocked cupboards, a working car, loving husband, healthy son, beautiful daughter-in-law, two energetic granddaughters, and news that grandbaby #3 was due in September. I had friends who called yet their outreaches were drowned out by sound waves of grief. Those pathetic, weary, half hearted attempts toward gratefulness slowly became steady drops to refill a dry Red Creek. Drip by drip, I weakly but consistently fought to move through grief by saying thank you for what I used to consider the most mundane provisions (i.e. carpeted floors, the light in the refrigerator, a flushing toilet, the smell of fresh mulch).

God used His sweet creativity to heal me through nature. He'd plant sweet visuals such as floppy-eared puppies tousling in fresh cut grass, or yellow butterflies "playing tag." He pointedly placed people in my path with words to assure me that sunnier times would return. These daily partings of Red Creeks and Red Rivers washed away some of the soul debris so I could keep swimming with my head above water. Earthly journeys promise trials and tribulations, but God supplies waders, umbrellas, and sometimes anchors and submarines for the Red Seas of life. His Word engulfs all the rules of the Red Sea.

PRAYING LIKE A WOODPECKER

Sometimes I feel like Dustin Hoffman's character in the movie *Rainman*. When highlights and lowlights of my day appear, I want to record those in my journal. The written recap serves as an elevator carrying my life's 'lessons and blessins', a pulley connecting my heart and actions.

One morning, I pictured God as the Elevator Operator as I rode His elevator cart up and down earth's floors. I was mid-visual when I heard a tap-tap-tapping on the gutter next door. Thinking it was our neighbor attaching the eaves spout, I returned to writing my elevator reflection. The drumming got louder so I figured the neighbor may have grabbed a larger tool to secure the gutter. I needed concentration to write so the time of persistent knocking seemed to intensify. I finally went outside to track the source of pattering. Instead of seeing our neighbor repairing his gutter, I saw a large woodpecker attacking the eave spout with its beak and flying to assail another section of pipe. I don't know how to decipher between male and female woodpeckers, but he or she repeatedly sacrificed its face to satisfy an unseen mission. I watched this headlong assault and simultaneously applauded and pitied the woodpecker's perseverance. It saddened me to know there wasn't a sustainable food source at the end of its work even if he (or she) punctured the gutter.

The innocent woodpecker became my feathered teacher who mirrored times of my life. In watching the bird knock on its rooftop drive-through window, I carried out food for thought. I share a woodpecker's style of approaching life when I'm hunting for answers. I knock on heaven's door, pound the rock, and seek shelter in the storm. At times, I walk around with a Teflon armor that causes truth to slide off my mental frying pan. I go through the motions of tap-tap-tapping in gutters that hold water but my tunnel vision holds nothing solid enough to withstand high winds.

Even more revealing is how I face plant into a gutter, fill my beak and head feathers with knowledge but disregard action. I become a dried-out skeleton crawling to a hollow door, convinced that if I knock heavily and frequently on the same opening, someone will answer. I've so worn myself out from endless pounding that I'm too tired to turn the door handle myself. I falsely believe I can bust-through to a break through by using enough determination. Persistence is crucial and prevails when the mission is in line with God's assignments.

From woodpecker to the man at Baal. For this story's details, please refer to John 5:2-7 in the Bible. I relate to this man waiting to be healed at the side of the pool. Sometimes I want someone *else* to help me into the healing water. I doubt my feeble words or actions are strong enough or perfect enough or polished enough to get God's attention. I wish someone *else* would answer my plea to guide me along directionless paths. Like the woodpecker, I show up for life to tap. Knocking louder or with more force is like asking for a larger bird with a stronger beak to unlock a food source. I end up running out of pecking power.

Jesus said in Matthew 18:2 that we must become like little children to experience the Kingdom of God. I interpret that scripture literally when my inner child switches into tapping overdrive. My childlike wonder desires to honk out a temper tantrum. I'd like to hide under someone else's feathers instead of picking up my nest and carrying it. Since I'm eating crow, I also confess that in the middle of life's tail winds, it's easier to flap my wings or beak about somebody else's concerns vs. claiming the promise that I'm a daughter of God.

After doing a mourning dove dance, a discussion starter game widened the perception of my wing span. Tig and I played this mind stretcher game for date night and the question on the card read, "If you could live your life as any Biblical character, who would you be and why?" Tig has been a longtime fan of the apostle Paul so I expected his answer to be Paul but instead it was Noah. Tig reasoned that he'd chance being flooded in Noah's yacht over Paul's multiple beatings, imprisonment, and starvation. I believe Tig's never-ending appetite and love for food was his deal breaker in choosing Noah over Paul. There's no biblical record that Noah went without a meal. Paul, on the other hand, talks about how he often starved so he could deliver Jesus' bread of life message.

We talked more about Noah and discussed what his neighbors may have thought about him building a structure with no blueprints in his yard. There hadn't been a drop of rain prior to what Noah heard from a 'source' nobody else saw. How many doctors at that time sat at stone conference tables in caves discussing this elderly man showing signs of dementia and hearing an unseen voice? How many comedians circa 2300 B.C. salivated for new material for their Men in Robes stand-up comic tour at the expense of Noah. Bob, the Builder, was child's play compared to this ark builder.

Tig and I bantered about other experiences Noah possibly faced during the ark-itecture. He completed the project even if his name wouldn't be in lights, or lanterns. We scanned Bible stories to find a character whose life held the least amount of trials. I appreciated Naomi's faithfulness to Ruth. I admired Gideon for leading an army after an angel found him flying under the radar in a winepress. I thought Shulamate was the one who had the world by the fig branches. She had a zeal for life, didn't appear intimidated by cultural norms, and married this hottie Solomon with wisdom oozing from his pores. Let me be Shulamate. Tig paused to think about my answer, and then simply asked, "Would you really want to be woman #701 after Solomon's previous 700 concubines?" OK Eder! Maybe Shulamate had forks in her family fig tree too.

As we travel from Biblical times to present day moral-of-the-story wrap up, we're hard pressed to find any Biblical characters who didn't struggle, experience grief, face tragedy and bloodshed. Each person had heart wrenching transitions that took them from wounded to warrior status, from puny to powerful. Each champion had internal battles to fight: addictions, fear, pride, selfishness, lust, greed, and comparison traps.

I realize God not only has His eye on the sparrow, He watches over the bird brains and woodpeckers in every life stage. He is my Wingman from field to flight!

WAIT FOR THE WAVES

What started out to be a book about random musings I had while running has escalated to Mud Run status. The path has traversed on somewhat of a mental marathon, filled with obstacles on its ten year slalom course (it's July 2018 so I may need to change the length of time taken on this path. Thankfully all races and running competitions don't extend the finish line after the starting shoot out).

People ask when I'm going to publish or wonder if I'm still writing because it was so long ago that I began this process. I plowed into a barbed wire section of writing this book. I became landlocked. What originally began in 2008 as a whimsical light read evolved into guiding insights and deeper revelations. Instead of waiting for perfect sailing conditions, I'm climbing into my writing chair kayak to dip one oar at a time until I finish this ocean of a manuscript.

SPIRITUAL DEPLOYMENT

Spiritual Deployment. These two words greeted my morning's sunrise. I experienced two and a half years of a spiritual deployment. What I thought was a rebirth in the silent retreat of 2014 turned out to be boot camp preparation. I sought God's face and I found light. With the intensity from the silent retreat, I expected that heat to sustain warmth to bask in long lasting rays. However, the war that followed resembled an internal Desert Storm! War heroes and military battles speak volumes of understanding. I had heard about soul awakening but until a two and a half year encounter with a desert, I was merely reading about those experiences. Now on the other side of a drought, I'm at a written intersection where I just want to copy the pages of my journal and insert them here. During one book revision, I grew exhausted reading about the two and a half year face plant. I deleted over 100 pages in one edit because in good conscience (vs. bad conscience?) I couldn't subject a reader to my Ecclesiastes theme of nothing new under the sun. I wanted to finish the book here with "blah blah blah, another person writes her memoir about desert walking until awakening. Who cares? Nuf said." The editors didn't agree so I plod along. I'd still rather stop here and listen to *your* story while we share some dark chocolate blueberries. I'd ask what pieces of my journey you can relate to. I crave hearing about the areas of this book where you are scream, "Christina, put stock in the dairy cows because this is downright cheesy! You can't possibly milk out these lessons anymore!" I ache for feedback, wondering if my book increases value to the reader or simply adds a bulk of paper to recycle.

I'm tempted to log off the computer and tackle other things on my agenda today. I'd rather be shopping for new underwear. My legs are stubbly but I don't want to shave with that single blade dull razor. I'm annoyed with the dollar store pens I just bought. I want to think about anything to divert this gritty writing juncture, to accomplish tasks that are less heavy than writing this deluge of enlightenment. I yearn to convey awakened wisdom without banging the Bible. I'd rather be dusting ceiling fans to avoid writing about faith without preaching. Someday, if you ever meet my sister Cathy, ask her to show you her "eat your beets" visual. Her "eat your beets" facial expression resembles my writing struggle. I'm only extending my painful writing struggle because I'm using the time to avoid pain through seemingly worthwhile distractions. Thinking how my writing job and Biblical Job are ironically spelled the same and mean the same thing in this moment. Both references involve waiting. Waiting to find a better job. Waiting until there is a job. Waiting for the end of the job day. In all this weight and wait, God sent a camel-sized message (carrier pigeons don't travel well in deserts). In my "God voice" I heard: "A job will come from people, joy will come from Me." Jobs have revolving doors. He remains my constant Door Keeper, even when I dead bolt the locks of my mind. I am to find joy IN the job.

With newfound momentum, I stuck out my neck to ask God, "So, what *new* job assignments do You want me to complete?" My answer wasn't to seek a new job, but to develop, persevere, finish the assignment He gave me in this book. Before new editing jobs and before new life coaching clients, I am to write this book to completion and publish it. I began this book in 2008 with a "someday I'll write that book" dream. A dream is only a dream unless there's action behind the words.

To end this gritty but finished chapter using the job and Job spelling reference, I use another group of homophones: Reign, rein, rain. God reign in my day, rein me in as You want, rain down Your perfect guidance.

Life's Too Short for Dull Razors, Cheap Pens, and Worn Out Underwear | Christina Eder

LIKE A BRIDGE OVER TROUBLED WATERS

I want to bridge these last chapters with energy that can only come from second-wind energy. There is no set amount of pages, there is no end to my thoughts, there is no finish line to indicate that the book is done, end of the road, game over. I want to leave this book on a runner's high, not a suffocated breath to neurotically expect every word to change every reader. I yearn to have every reader close this book (preferably at the end and not here) with at least one sentence that added value to their run, no matter what pace they run. The following reflections are votive size candle lessons that have lit my path. They have guided me toward more whole hearted living. Wholly living requires me to have continual open heart surgery that fixes, repairs, celebrates blood pumping, and muscles moving. This potpourri of stories has jogged life moments of fitness walks, fun runs, sprints, and recovery from distance courses. It's been a relay for life.

We found a solution that created more peaceful transitions between school, work, and home. Our son has since moved out, married, and has a family, but Tig and I continue using our family's "no wake zone guideline." When another person came home, we gave that person a ten to fifteen minute window of space. Apart from emergencies, we greeted 'the-just-got-home-person' with a quick enthusiastic hello then gave them room to decompress. Mail, messages, or questions waited until dinner when everyone had their 10-15 minutes quiet break.

This ritual allowed the person to transition from one role to another: i.e. manager to father; administrator to wife; student to son. It offered a chance to take personal inventory about what they needed most to show up for family dinner more refreshed from whatever their day brought. Those first minutes invited a check-in with self to determine if a short nap, bathroom break, water, closed door reflection, read time, prayer, or walk was most needed.

Within this window of respect, we also asked each person to call before they headed home. The phone call wasn't to initiate a debriefing of the day, but as a courtesy call that there would be some new waves on the waterfront called home. Their ship was coming in and we wouldn't barge into each other's wake. This locked up turbulent waters with a lot less dam(n) in family conversations! I've gone overboard with nautical puns.

Our son, now 27 years old, is married with three daughters. He called to share how the no wake zone time set the tone for a more relaxing evening and he was going to start that with his family. During his call of walk down memory lane, Todd reminded me how we frequently said halt. HALT was our acronym code when one of us was 'flying less than sunny skies.' If we were Hungry, Angry/Anxious, Lonely, Tired, we addressed that before we spoke. Todd remembers hearing HALT often so we recognize we needed frequent reminders. HALT became a pseudo life insurance policy because spoken words don't receive a do-over or retraction. He is captain of his family ship anchored to a stellar first mate wife. It is their turn to discover what propels their family toward the best sailing conditions.

A NET WORTH

During times of waiting, I sometimes feel like I'm walking around in a stunned daze or comatose state. I often impatiently pause for breakthrough or change and somehow, the song *100 Bottles of Beer* pops a top in my head. This monotonous little diddy has become a traditional road trip theme song. Long bus trips invoke one self-proclaimed choir leader to begin, "100 bottles of beer on the wall, 100 bottles of beer…" Many people enthusiastically join the song leader. The first two or three bottles are frivolous and the chorus line remains strong. After the fourth and fifth bottle, people experience an auditory buzz. They secretly hope the song leader will pass out. If the lyric masters make it to the sixth or seventh bottle, many travelers holler, "last call." I don't recall any trip where I was subjected to singing or listening to anything beyond bottle #83. That may be a journal entry under gratitude…

Belly up to the bar, there is a purpose for this grueling song in the story. I started a season of several part-time jobs in June 2015 and by October 2016 I wondered if my career wisdom became intoxicated. The decision to leave a full time job with benefits was wholeheartedly sound. I still believe it was the right choice. However, my glee club spark to continue the live version of the 100 Bottles of Beer dance significantly declined.

I wrote in my journal: "In my fierce exploration for purpose, I've lost the sense of purpose. I crave to take the next step but don't know where the finish line is. Where do I even step?" Caught mid-lamentation, I was guided with, "Do everything *with* purpose and that will *be* a purpose."

Shortly after that spirit alignment, I recognized how I was imitating the Israelites after they began their journey toward the Promised Land. They had forgotten, or repressed, the cow pie conditions of their homeland, yet they wanted to return. They walked toward freedom but yearned to run back to known territory and the once-considered daily grind. Because they didn't know what a promised land looked like, they murmured and complained about pressing forward. Just like the beer bottle song, the Israelites forgot the original sense of their Promised Land adventure. I forgot the enthusiasm of my original quest to explore a potpourri of jobs.

I relish quiet. I require vast amounts of solitude. I find solace more calming when there is a specific destination to work toward. Prior to setting my own working schedule, solo time used to be a nurturing balm. Now it mocked me with a deafening hollowness. I was in that 83 bottles of beer on the wall phase. At least in that annoying but catchy tune, I know there's an end when one lone bottle remains on the shelf. Waiting for directional breakthrough looked like watching dust accumulate around each bottle taken from the shelf. No matter how often I took, shifted, threw, and recycled my bottles of life, I still saw the same shelf, same brands, same Norm at the end of the bar. Cheers.

A CAST OF CHARACTERS

One of my friends is a theatre teacher. She's part of my small circle in which I can confidentially bare my soul without crawling into my protective shell. Sara encourages perceptional twists to offset my original perspective and greets change as her call to action. She tenaciously lives her days with opening night wonder matched with closing night stamina.

I've watched Sara prepare for productions and she seamlessly adapts costume changes and stage set-ups with a keen sense of resiliency. Some rehearsals and performances are spot-on according to script. More often, unforeseen circumstances make cameo appearances and she maintains unedited composure.

During one of her rehearsals, I recognized I needed to allow *and* invite God to rewrite my life script on an hourly basis. I wanted to replace my laser pointed beam with a clear floodlight to shine God's stage presence. Unknowingly, through her profession and lifestyle, Sara inspired me to redesign my (mind) set. I have witnessed her select and develop a cast of less than exceptionally talented performers and create dynamic plays. She courts the most unlikely-to-live-to-the-end-of-one-rehearsal personalities and marries them under a spotlight of happily- ever-after (at least on stage).

I adapted Sara's style in diversifying her casts, especially in the marital venue. One person can fill a lot of anything, but *every*thing? Tig is the lead role in my life but had I placed unhealthy pressure on him to excel in every role of my life? That question led to a candid marital conversation about different hats Tig wore in our marriage. He is too kind to admit he sometimes feels like Mrs. Doubtfire minus the costume changes. I interpreted his gentle smile as a yes and decided to add more cast on my life's stage.

Other crew members needed to be part of our troupe on this tour called Life. I made a list of people who would help me show up for life as the best version of myself. As circumstances change, specific people may rotate in my life but each vital role remains filled. My fully staffed cast encourages wholeness plus provides the added benefit of releasing Tig from unnecessary strain of playing more roles than God does in my life.

I have chosen this troupe for Tour de Earthly Life. Some of these characters are exactly that…characters!

Comedian: Someone who understands I horse laugh at trips, slips, and falls. All humorous convulsions immediately stop if there is blood. The comedian is naturally quick witted, slightly sarcastic without being snarky.

Accountability Partner: Someone who invites me to share ideas and dreams then follows-up on those goals with genuine interest.

Prayer Partner: A sister in Christ with faithful coverage, not someone who will just pat my hand with a carte blanche, "I'll pray for you."

Motivator/Cheerleader: This person enthusiastically says, "Christina, you can do this! I support you even if I'm not remotely fascinated in your desire to go hang gliding."

Dream Chaser: An energized individual willing to partner in planning a trip or activity *and* show up! Someone who converts their spoken promise to action.

Fashion Consultant : Someone forward enough to gently notice my attire needs an upgrade and offer to share their honest opinion of clothing styles when we do the four-letter "s" word (rhymes with flop).

Listener: An attentive person not easily distracted, especially by phone and screen time. This has become the toughest role to cast. I find it increasingly difficult finding people with sufficient respect to allow someone to finish a sentence before interrupting. It's been equally complicated to connect with someone surgically attached to their phone. Cut! Back to my cast listing…

Tear Whisperer: I typically journal my way through adversity and limit my tear duct workouts to non-public places. Should unpredictable crying occur, I'm grateful to the Tear Whisperer who does not rush to grab tissues at the first sign of watering eyes. This person also allows me ample time to tearfully express pain without rushing to offer their solution to my situation.

Spiritual Director: A wise, older, seasoned person with a wide range of life experiences. Someone who blends directness with compassion and not lamely appease my emotional tangents. I'd rather learn to get to heaven in a more laser focused way than using my methods to learn lessons on repeat play.

I'm grateful for my current cast members scripted into this screen shot of life. I'm anticipating future troupes to fill supporting roles as new scenarios are written.

SOCIAL BUTTERFLY OR SOCIAL MOSQUITO?

I bask in delightful introversion and feel most alive on solo missions. Understanding I also need and want my tiny circle of people, I factored my hidden extroverted self into part of a day's equation. I called a few friends I haven't connected with lately and discovered a twist to my introverted default. Instead of being drained, I felt energized after the calls, especially when a friend exclaimed, "It's good to hear your voice! I'm used to everyone just texting anymore." This friend laughed when she followed her comment with, "Well, you are one of the flip phone survivors so I understand why you don't text often." When I called a couple of family members they answered the phone with a hesitated tremble. Their first question was, "Are you ok? When I saw your number come up, I was worried something bad happened since you never call."

I choose not to participate in mass media communication so sometimes I wonder if I present myself like Rip Van Winkle. Some people tell me I'm isolating myself by not keeping up with what goes on in others' daily lives. Instead of feeling like an outsider apathetically looking on, I value being mindfully present in whatever intersects my everyday path. I struggle with keeping up with my own Joneses and watch how people become stressed or excited when they stream updates about other Joneses. Friendly smiles, chats at the grocery store, library, and other public places is my preferred method of social media

Social media confuses me because I was raised not to gossip and if someone wanted to share news on their own, that was up to only them. Re-tweeting, re-posting, and forwarding messages debunk those foundational teachings. We have privacy guidelines, HIPAA laws, and passwords to get into anything more secure than Wal-Mart so to me, social media seems like an oxymoron. Maybe I'm rebelling against the social butterfly craze. I see personal mass communication as somewhat of an electronic mosquito rather than a social butterfly.

From my Extroverted Lady's Day Out phone calls, it was refreshing to hear a live voice instead of reading typed messages but I miss conversations that dive beyond surface level talk. Some of those phone calls began with dialogue about people we both knew. I hadn't asked for other people's updates, but was informed about what x, y, and z was doing based on social media sites. Instead of blatantly saying I didn't care to know about x, y, and z, I asked, "What is the most exciting thing *you've* learned or done this week?" Sadly, I was met with the sound of crickets and sensed an uncomfortable fidgeting on the other end of the line. I wanted to lightly steer the conversation from a gossip tone toward discovering her undertakings. She simply answered, "Oh I've just been so busy." My gentle steer escalated to a grinding gear shift when I excitedly asked, "Yeah? Busy with what?" Instead of recapping her activity, I was met with an awkward stammering. She said she didn't have much to tell other than work and house chores.

I'm surprised to hear how people feel ostracized or empty even though they are connected on social media and networking groups. I'm not conducting a debate between social or anti-social media but I found three correlating statistics in the July 23, 2018 *FIRST for Women* magazine. Page 40 has a quick take about how Americans would spend an extra hour in their day. 91% listed "unplugged from technology." Six pages later, from the same issue, a quote from *Psychological Review* stated that 90% of people didn't want to know about negative future events. My question was why then do people voluntarily read every breaking news article? Finally, another quick take from the same magazine in the same issue, credit *Dream Dinners*: "What gets in the way of family dinner?" Rushing to eat due to schedule conflicts: 33%; TV and computer 31%; cell phones at the table 24%; difficulty engaging kids in conversation 13%. Originally I typed, "Duh!" Knowing my editor would cut that response, I modified, "And we need three statistics to state the decline of social interaction as if this is riveting news?" My best graceful tact concluded, "Am I missing something?" From my nearly unplugged vantage point, I see much of networking to be an expense instead of an investment of time.

To me, social media has taken time that was once used for arts, fishing, sports, music, crafting, hunting, reading to children, walking, breathing without a screen in your face...whoops. Now I see more time being used online, watching what others do and say. I also don't understand how people are drawn to reading about what others say on social networks, but in face-to-face conversations, distracted listening speaks volumes. A reader may post a comment about this. I'll be outside running to update my mileage log instead of Facebook.

STIRRING

During a chocolate craving, I tried imagining what my walk with Jesus looked like this past year. Never underestimate the power of sugary carbs to connect two seemingly unrelated items. Jesus and chocolate are related. Different levels of love, but love nonetheless.

I pictured myself as a bowl of dry chocolate chip cookie ingredients. I am flour, baking soda, brown sugar, salt, and white sugar sitting in a large mixing bowl. Life slowly heats the margarine, inviting me to soften parts of my heart. Melted butter drips around my soul, encouraging me to mix warm spirit with dry clumps of ingredients. God patiently waits while His Holy Spoon (or Holy Spirit) gently stirs my soul.

Logic is grateful for His slow gentle stirring of new life coming together. My flesh wonders why He doesn't speed up the process and crank that industrial size mixer up a notch. He has the power of a Hobart mixer, but chose to use an Amish cooking method. If He promoted me to my next assignment early, a warning label may indicate, "Raw ingredients. Do not eat uncooked dough." Thanks (written in sarcastic font) to the scorching heat from a 2 ½ year spiritual desert, I've experienced a preheated soul, but raw sections of my growth require more baking.

One missing ingredient can transform a Tollhouse recipe into a 'Troll-house' disaster. If you've ever diminished the importance of ½ tsp of baking soda, you soon realize how that seemingly minor elimination alters the cookie. Christina M. Eder, who wishes to remain anonymous, may have read about a friend who overlooked that baking soda detail….

… So here I sit with ingredients, mixer, oven. Life experience and smaller at the time trials have been part of my baking process. I needed lower temperature build-ups to gradually reach a 350' cooking mark. That gradual incline is God's gracious mercy holding a steady hand on the oven dial.

As seasoned bakers can testify, the quality of pans is vital for superior baking results. If my heart is a baking sheet what does it look like? If I'm a blackened pan, what benefit would life's best circumstances be if my motives are self-seeking? If I show up for life with worn-out Teflon coating, no amount of cooking spray will protect me from burning. Like a properly prepared baking stone, I need God to lay a solid foundation for my next step, or at least my next shuffle.

The cookie smell is part of the delicious process of baking. Only during the last few minutes in the oven do cookies start filling the house with a cozy scent. It's a waiting game toward the coveted smell wafting beyond the kitchen. If I open the oven door to remove the cookies before the baking process is finished, the dough falls apart. I'd also be breaking the first commandment written on a baking stone: never eat raw cookie dough.

During times of spiritual bed rest, I slowly engage these lighter comparisons for heavier life teachings. I've learned about life through the creation of baked treats. Sometimes that's how the cookie crumbles.

THIS IS ONLY A TEST

I was listening to the radio and smack dab in the middle of a catchy little tune, that deafening alert sound blurted across the air waves. I thought the signal was to broadcast breaking news or weather alert, but a recorded message followed. The Emergency Broadcasting Station was conducting a routine test. I wished EBS tests were conducted between songs instead of when I was mid-belt-it-out-at-the-top-of-my-lungs chorus. I waited for Mr. Canned Radio Announcer Voice to finish his reassuring comments telling us the breakup between song and singer was only a test.

That pause caused me to reflect on how I frequently truck along life's highway and something will jump in the way of my Plan A. The interruption may be a person, traffic pattern, job task, phone call, or a myriad of other distractions. Like the Emergency Broadcast Station alert, interruptions are jolts from my routine, but most times, there isn't an actual emergency.

How could I respond differently if I considered self-defined interruptions as "this is only a test of my inner reaction system"? Similar to a "count to ten" delayed response, if I immediately reminded myself that distractions are only a test, my 911 reactions would diminish. For example, if a boss added an unexpected project to my duties, I can quickly say "this is only a test." "This is only a test" is limited to internal dialogue before responding to said manager, not as an automatic recommendation. Typically, my unexpected events don't require a call to 911. No fire? No medical emergency? No robbery? No assault? If I answer no to any or all of these questions, I'm learning to reframe my interruption as an unplanned assignment. I write this as a self-reminder that interruptions often resemble a pop quiz rather than a test. Tests are usually administered with forewarning.

Outside of an emergency, I started declaring self-defined interruptions as, "this is only a pop quiz." It's a pop quiz of character. It's a creative assessment to respond more calmly. It's a flexibility exercise. It's an exam to make sure I anchor tighter during life's intense wind storms.

Countless times, I've experienced these test alerts and jumped into flight or fight mode. Collectively, I've spent endless hours loading my verbal pistol because I reacted as if a catastrophic event occurred when the encounter was only a test. How much wasted energy have I used to bolt toward my comfort zone instead of waiting for further instruction after the alert? In the Grand Canyon of events, most of my emergencies wouldn't register as a drizzle, much less the flood of response I pour out.

Today, I'll incorporate a "this is only a test" response. If the circumstance *is* an actual emergency,

I trust that I'll engage situational tethers to weather whatever storm. I'll strive to listen more closely to that small still voice.

THE WONDER OF CHRISTMAS

This chapter's original title was *The Wander of Christmas*. If I still wrote letters to Santa, I'd notice that none of the gifts I want this year can be wrapped. Nothing I need can be packaged in a holly jolly elf bag.

The irony of this reflection is how much I sound like my Dad. As kids, every year we'd ask Dad what he wanted most for Christmas. The answer was the same each year. He'd tilt his head back with a contemplative expression that we came to know as partially joking, partially a wiser man leaving a legacy of values. He'd sit in his chair and offer a faraway look before he answered, "What I want most is year-long peace, wisdom, contentment…" At this point, we knew his canned response so we'd interject, "NO Dad! We're serious!" He'd gently smile and say, "I'm serious too." He'd continue, "I'd like more joy, understanding…" "No! Dad, we mean something we can buy you at the store!" He'd shift his upward glance to our eye level and continue, "In addition to peace, wisdom, joy, understanding, I'd also like love, more time with family…" We'd roll our eyes and go ask Mom for ideas. As the years went on, we'd preface our "what do you want for Christmas" query with, "Dad, *other* than peace, wisdom, joy, love, and all that other stuff you always say, what do you want for Christmas?" He'd smile when he'd say he appreciated that we quickly remembered all of his wish list. He'd lean back further in his chair and say, "You know you're right. All that peace, wisdom, joy, and love is great, but this year, I thought of something I'd really like to add." We'd brace ourselves for the big reveal.

We readied ourselves to be the first to run out and buy that one thing he was about to disclose. He'd smile that same contemplative smile, "I knew you were going to ask me this question again. I know I need something more important than peace, wisdom, joy, and love. This year I noticed I lost some gentleness. I need soft tenderness to rub out some rough abrasiveness in this hard head of mine." We unanimously greeted his answer with a loud, "DAD! No really!" To which he'd assure us, "Yes, really. Gentleness is what I need most this year."

Later, through Bible studies and Dad's Christmas wishes, we realized he was listing the fruits of the spirit (Galatians 5:22-23). Who would have thought Dad and Paul the author of Galatians had the same Christmas list?

Fast forward from the 1970's...As the primary breadwinner, Dad had physical wants and needs but he taught us values in eternal priorities. I'm sitting this Christmas season with a few material needs that could be store bought, but I'm most needy of peace, joy, guidance, wise discernment, and aligning my talents with a passionate purpose.

The star on top of our Christmas tree is lit with my light of understanding that I'm pointing my attention toward material gains. God frequently reminds me, "Be still and know that I'm God" but my spiritual hearing aids were turned off. I notice I spend much time scrambling, not stilling. I operate under forced worldly logic instead of flowing with Holy Spirit guidance. I carry buckets of ice water instead of trusting God to faithfully pour His warm water over me. I plant, water, fertilize (sometimes spreading abundant piles of manure) instead of letting the land lay fallow. I fan flames instead of simply sitting around God's campfire watching His gentle glow.

Thankfully my spiritual snooze bar clicked on and I woke to witness myself walking toward the self-sabotaging landmine. With sleepy eyes, I was gifted with childhood Christmas memories intersecting with adult Christmas message understanding.

Going back to 1970's Christmas Eve, minus the part-in-the-middle-braided hair and monogrammed sweater. Our family set out cookies and milk for Santa. My siblings woke Christmas morning to find cookie remains and maybe a light ring around the milk glass. We'd run to the tree with anticipation of Santa's gifts. Pajama clad, before Mom and Dad woke up, we'd try to guess what may be in each package. It seemed that Mom and Dad slept later on Christmas than any other morning. My brother and sister talked about what they wanted most and looked for a wrapped gift that possibly matched something from their wish list.

When we couldn't wait any longer, we'd go to Mom and Dad's bedroom to see how much longer before we could open gifts. Dad's waiting ritual was just as deliberate and drawn out as his contemplative Christmas gift answer. Looking back, that waiting period from Christmas morning eye opening to gift opening seems like a snap. Maybe 30 years from today, I'll lightheartedly recall, "that 2 ½ year waiting between 2014 and 2017 sure went by quickly."

The tie-in between 1970 as a child and my now adult self is how I trusted Santa to stop at our house. It didn't matter if there was an address change or no house chimney, I trusted my parents when they said Santa had a way of knowing exactly where to find us. I need to trust that Jesus is already with me. At times, I feel like I'm behind a dark curtain, but it's Jesus covering me as He prepares me for His unveiling.

Unlike Santa, Jesus' visits aren't limited to Christmas time. He is faithful no matter if I'm naughty or nice. Do I set out prayers like I set out cookies and milk? Like the gloppy frosting and excessive cinnamon candied cookies, my prayers aren't professional decorator quality and they're found in the day-old bakery sections of my heart. Like Santa, I picture Jesus picking up my messy cookie and milk prayers, taking a bite, and smiling in

His grandfatherly Santa way. He may even throw in a ho-ho-ho as if to knowingly say, "Oh child, have I got a surprise for you!"

My journal is the grown-up version of a Santa letter. Instead of using the kitchen table as a setting for letter writing, cookies and milk, I'm learning to figuratively leave my requests at His feet. My altar becomes the chimney to which Jesus has 24-7 access if my heart flue is open. I picture going to bed with peaceful wonder of Jesus staying in my house as I sleep. When I awake, I am assured of presents and His Presence as He teaches with new mercies every day. There is also promise that there may be pain in the night, but joy comes in the morning. I daily fight the waffle between human belief of who God really is and what He says He'll do. As a daughter of God, He tells me to expect gifts (James 1:17).

Each minute could be viewed as a surprise wrapped by the Ultimate Gift Giver. Some minutes hold a package of anticipation. Some moments are so noticeably wrapped in joy. Uncovering gifts may include supernatural peace, a new lesson, refreshing smile, wonder, laughter, or an uplifting phone call.

As a child, I didn't question *if* Santa would leave gifts. I questioned *which* gifts he was leaving. Beyond December 25, am I waking each day with anticipation, wonder, and *expectation* that Jesus already dropped off a warehouse worth of presents while I slept? Circumstances from the previous day often dictate how I greet a new day. A quote from Anne Ortlund, "Pain is God's beautiful gift to make us lean harder on Him when He knows we need it."

Instead of dragging trials and tribulations into today, I refocus to thank God for all the gifts I unwrapped yesterday. With praise for yesterday's laughter, cozy bed, heated car, soft carpet, and running water. I ask Him to point out any gifts He freely gave me that I left unopened or unused from yesterday such as using the smile He designed only for me. Was I appreciative of my meals? Did I half-listen with one ear, even though He gifted me with two sharp ears? I also include Dad's Christmas list into my praiseworthy offerings: peace, joy, patience, fortitude, temperance....

THE QUIET REVOLUTION

In addition to peace, joy, patience, fortitude, and temperance, I need and want quiet. As I've grown older, my spirit requires more quiet than ever before. Quietness is no longer a luxury for special occasions, but as vital to my health as my lungs. One of my 21st century heroines is Susan Cain, author of *Quiet. The power of Introverts in a World That Can't Stop Talking*. This woman unknowingly granted me permission to release the Mt. Rushmore sized boulder on my spirit. She is the founder of *Quiet Revolution* where she is expanding her mission to incorporate the value of low levels of sensory stimulation. Susan Cain and her website writers have given me freedom to not only embrace, but love less noise.

I grew up being taught to "use your inside voice." I repeatedly heard there is a time for noise, there is a time for quiet. We didn't chatter in church before services, we didn't converse in the library, and we didn't talk when adults were speaking. Restaurants used to simply house tables, chairs, food, workers, and other patrons. Sometimes, we hit the jackpot and a restaurant offered a box of four colors and paper placemat to color at the table while waiting for our food. When Tig and I began dating, we discovered a bounty about each other through dinner conversations. We asked about each other's opinions and caught up on life while enjoying a meal cooked and served by someone else. The beauty of conversation was asking a question and hearing the answer without your ear touching the other person's lips to be heard.

Now restaurants have large screens tuned in to different stations in every corner while music blares over multiple televisions. There are stage shows for customers celebrating anything from birthdays to buying goldfish. Tig and I no longer have talking interaction when we go out to eat. Up until this year, I suffered (somewhat) silently with the physical assault of TV's, loud overhead music, and show stealing children who often aren't taught about their inside voice. There's a barrage of cell phone conversations toppling over patrons talking, ring tones going off, and a server trying to clarify an order in between the non-stop auditory deluge. This modern day noise leaves my stomach in turmoil, crushing out any appetite I had prior to walking into the food circus.

In her Ted Talk, Susan Cain points out that prior to the Industrial Revolution we were primarily an agrarian society. People had jobs, workers had space, and they were around other people, but worked more independently. Open concept offices, ice breakers, more team approaches, and shared desks leave limited places to collect unique and individual thoughts. With this constant interaction creativity can be stymied because of limited time to solo digest and process ideas. Some might counter that frequent interactions create a larger melting pot for possible solutions. For an introvert, an open concept working situation can be nerve wracking.

I believe standard office jobs would better thrive if the staff resembled a musical band. Each musician has a duty to learn, practice, and cultivate their instrumental skill. After a set time of individual rehearsal, the band gathers to play the song. Based on the sound of the band as a whole unit, the musicians then disengage to practice and polish until the band meets again. If it was mandated that all band members stay in the same room to rehearse, there may be drum sticks flying, strings wrapped around more than the guitar's neck, and vocal exchange requiring much studio editing and voice over. There's respect and expectation for solo space to strengthen the entire band's work.

Team sports operate under a similar school of thought. Each player develops their throw, jump shot, technique, and stance before coming together as a team to play a game. Even during practice, players are allowed space as they hone their skill. They work best when there's independent exercises and individual coaching prior to collective team effort.

A theatre troupe has ample amounts of individual script memorizing before they gather on stage. Each actor, dancer, and cast requires their own space and time to create a well crafted performance.

Through Susan Cain's *Quiet* book, I understand why middle school sleepovers were a disappointment for me as a low sensory stimulated introvert. At 10:00 my social energy quotient was spent and I was ready to sleep (hence, the term *sleep*over?). I could have fielded "you're such a party poop" teasing if I had disengaged from the group to go somewhere to read. Instead, I stayed among the seventh grade girls. Their random laughter outbursts and shouting over loud music became painful sensory overload. Remaining with the crowd opened me up to the girls asking why I stopped talking and why my ears were red. One of the more outspoken girls jeered how I looked like I was ready to cry. I let the crowd believe I was homesick because I didn't recognize why I was shutting down.

I thought introversion was a "deficiency" and I carried that assumption to high school and college. Class group projects simulated being thrown head first into a metal locker. The majority of time spent on a class project felt wasted because there was ample input with insignificant output. I rarely got invited to high school or college parties after word quickly spread about me leaving social gatherings by 9:00. One Monday, I overheard a classmate say, "I thought Christina would be more fun. We asked her to come to X's house Friday night because we figured she'd be the life of the party but she completely closed up. She's livelier at school than a party." Ironically I'm frequently categorized an excellent team player, but prefer assembling my portion alone before connecting it with the larger endeavor.

My reserved tendencies manifested in my first jobs as babysitter. I enjoyed the jobs with one, maybe two children. I preferred caring for older children because they could talk and reason. I related to their age-leveled games because there was an objective ahead of imaginative play. Older children also held substantial conversations beyond make believe stories and knock-knock jokes. It was exhausting to feign interest in younger children rhyming games, or re-enact scenarios adapted for action figures or Barbie land. I wanted to charge parents an additional cost for each time a child began any version of, "Miss Christina, let's pretend that …."

When I worked at Pizza Hut, most co-workers requested busier shifts because there was more tip money. I preferred a slow steady pace so I could serve each group more completely, one at a time. I worked undesirable shifts when the restaurant was "dead" so I wasn't subjected to the juke box and didn't absorb the congested hype of crowds. My extroverted co-workers didn't understand why I willingly worked more hours for equal, sometimes less, tip money. Once again, I accepted the lie that I was an outsider looking at the insider life.

The book *Quiet* "spoke volumes" in pursuit of understanding my preference around solo hobbies, minimal home décor, and smaller churches. My spirit yearns to hear my inside voice. Susan Cain also created the *Quiet Revolution* website. Between her research and the website authors, *Quiet Revolution* has become a personal version of my bible. Luke 5:16 teaches that Jesus often retreated from the crowds to hear from His heavenly Father. "As often as possible Jesus withdrew to out-of-the-way places for prayer" (Luke 5:16 TM). Jesus' love for quiet is confirmed, "while it was still night, way before dawn, He got up and went out to a secluded spot and prayed (Mark 1:35 TM). If I'm striving to be more like Jesus every day, frequent space and quiet times is powerful discipline.

I'm smiling as I write the next incredibly unmistakable observation. For forty years, I honed my resume to tailor to careers that I had no desire to fit into. I applied for jobs that paid the bills and met dreams. Paying bills and having dirty green paper to achieve dreams are good things. Trading every fiber of my joy and life calling in exchange for money has turned out to not be a good thing.

There are no less than fifty historic examples of my try-to-fit-the-job-market-mold. When newspaper job ads were the search engine, I paid close attention to the Sunday listing of careers. That edition of the paper had the most job listings and greatest variety. From newspaper to college campus job boards to internet, I talked myself into the most promising paycheck that made sense to the world. I sold myself into offices and job sites that paid for material existence but I wasn't earning a living.

During 2014-2017, my Desert Years, I listed specific perfect job conditions. I prefer quiet work settings that interact with people on a one-to-one capacity. I'd like a company that requires a neat dress code but doesn't expect employees to buy trendy clothes or wear a business suit. Coming from someone whose talents lie in areas outside of shopping or fashion, I vote for an adult adaptation of Garanimals. I'd like to simply pair a shirt with a raccoon emblem with a raccoon emblem on slacks. I'd be able to determine my outfit by matching a frog decal on a blouse to a frog decal on a skirt. This would eliminate my opening line, "Does this outfit match?" or "Is this style outdated?"

Back to near perfect job situations…I can work in an office but with the updated version of open door policy, I cringe. I've toured businesses using no wall approaches, with people close enough to hear each other breathe. Breathing is a great thing. As a runner I appreciate breath. If I'm unable to have my own office for an 8-10 hour work day, at least give me a breathing *room*.

I continued listing ideal working conditions and then the solution hit me. Flexibility, short commute, income, purposeful mission, sparsely populated office, prioritize a variety of deadlines, business casual dress, creativity, reading, teaching, editing, encouraging, continuing education. I interrupted myself. "So, Christina, you're looking for a job as a *writer*? A writer! A writer? You mean to do something I love? To use my favorite hobby and volunteer outlet and get paid to do those? How can writing be a real job if it's something I enjoy? Oh Archie! What a novel concept worthy of a Pulitzer Prize!

The writing has been on the wall for nearly four decades. As a child, I loved word searches, Scrabble, crossword puzzles, reading, listening to stories. My mom kept a story I wrote in second grade. The teacher had given me three blank pages to write any story I chose. I printed my plot on both sides of three pages. Some people dread and procrastinate on large written assignments. I was that student who completed ten page papers ahead of time and used writing lab times to struggle through five math problems. Random ponder: as a lover of word languages, "simple math problem" sounds like an oxymoron. It can't be a problem if it's simple, especially when it comes to numbers. Back from ponder point. In eighth grader, I toured our high school newspaper room and could hardly wait for middle school graduation so I could enter high school journalism. My favorite homework was writing a column for our school newspaper and typing yearbook stories while other classmates met other deadlines.

My original college major was journalism however I was swayed by other people's educational plan for my life and graduated with a business administration degree. I bought the logical approach that I could use my writing in any business job. I permitted myself to be defined by others as "someone too nice to write in a dog-eat-dog job field." I felt trapped in the wrong book of business. After graduation, my heart wanted to write but my stomach needed to eat so I looked for jobs that locked me into a virtual safety deposit box.

To save some trees of details, skip past years of inwardly dying at sterile jobs. Our church needed someone to write about volunteers working behind the scenes that many people weren't aware of. They chose me to author these stories and I rekindled a writing flame. I fanned the fire of desire and bought books about starting writing and publishing businesses. In those books, readers were cautioned of downsides in a writing career. Other than marketing and accounting, those downsides sounded like upsides to me. I wondered if I really was as quirky as people told me.

I read testimonies about people quitting their "real jobs" in pursuit of writing despite fear, no guarantees of work or money. I've spent years silently cheering those courageous authors and questioned why *everyone* wouldn't want to be a writer. Was I naïve?

Fast forward between revelation and transformation. I initially harbored regret about twenty plus years of misplaced energy. Fear around tax laws, bookkeeping, and government forms delayed my writing destiny. Instead of taking my concerns to a business accountant or financial professional for advice, I built a conservative job market resume. That long detour around the Freeway of Fear led me to job experiences that developed wisdom. The careers that held nothing related to writing were opportunities to practice integrity in sometimes less than honest work situations. There are uncountable ways I gained character and virtue through humility. Instead of a book review of looking back with regrets, I'm looking forward with tenacity to redeem those years and write with verve.

I've considered renaming this book, *"A Head from Behind: a look at life with 20/20 hindsight.* The cover would have a before and after photo of me wearing my glasses. In the before picture, I'm wearing glasses on my face. In the after picture, I'm wearing glasses on my (ahem) 'other end'. I'm crafting the rest of my life around my call to write, literally craving to weave words. I've been educated in schools where writing is deeply intertwined in every subject. I've published in smaller venues. I'm living when quality writing has declined (including my quality at times), self-publishing is acceptable, and manual typewriters are a piece of history. I also bring twenty additional years of experience to share.

I can't murmur about pasty white skin if I never step out in the sun. If there's an itch, scratch it. To some, an author's life sounds lonely, uncertain, tedious, enormously taxing on discipline. To me, those are gritty job features that send my spirit into written bulldozing, remodeling, and crafting heaven. Write on!

MUSINGS FROM MY PERSONAL JOURNAL

Part of my personal growth plan this year included reviewing the past 3 years of my journal. I'm looking for behavior patterns, thought musings, lessons learned, creative thoughts, random things I've heard. I've gotten unexpected joy in this inventory process so I tabbed them "I gotta remember this." These are what I consider my best ponderings of 2014-2017. Each entry may serve as a future book. Each fragment may develop into another collection of essays. For now I'm writing these as a time capsule during my 2014-2017 earthly journey.

While I'm journaling, I sometimes ramble or write in unfinished sentences. The grammar structure isn't perfect, punctuation may not be proper, but I share these blips with hopes that you can relate or they provide inspiration in some way. They are delivered as is with no warranty:

*Pen and paper are my two non-judgmental, no charge counselors. Write it out, wait it out, wear it out.

*What if I worked as if God is my CEO? Because He owns the world and provides everything to live in it He's already my CFO. How can I learn to trust Him more as my accountant, hiring coach, marketer, recruiter? I draw from God's endless bank of grace, peace, time, energy, hope, wisdom all day long. My deposits need to include praise for each minute He is in service…always!

*Help me be a light to others as a glowing campfire, not a wildfire.

*Scripture teaches that we are to forgive seven times seventy times. How many times has God thrown me a grace and mercy card? Much more than 7 x 70! Help me be that generous with forgiving others!

*I'm running into a struggle where I'm bracing myself against an unknown heavy instead of *em*bracing myself for something light.

*Show me the balance between my natural introversion/desire for quiet and stretching myself to be a blessing to others.

*Thank you: Max Lucado teaching about how God keeps thorns in our sides so we rely on Him solely and remain humble. These thorns can be anything from anxiety to people to health to finances. The greater our weakness, the stronger His power.

*In praise for making a Need to Do list and a Want to Do list. I commit to choosing a few from both lists so I can balance productivity with creativity each day. I gain satisfaction when I soak through recreation and serve through perspiration. I show up for life when I experience both sides of the spectrum every day.

*From a plaque I received as the last gift from a friend before he passed away:

EACH DAY TAKE TIME TO:

WORK: it is the price of success

PLAY: it is the secret of perpetual growth

THINK: it is the source of power

READ: it is the fountain of wisdom

PRAY: it is a conversation with God

LAUGH: it is the music of the soul

LISTEN: it is the pathway to understanding

DREAM: it is the hitching your wagon to a star

WORSHIP: it is the highway of reverence

LOVE: it is a gift of God

*Help me break down my fears of moving forward before analysis paralysis causes my courage to atrophy. I'm worried about use of time, heart desires, life management in general. Recognizing that I don't necessarily need approval from others, but I'm subconsciously waiting for other people's permission before I take a new or another step?!

*Praise: seeing how my love for baking becomes a teaching tool about balance, consistency, replacing ingredients. I can substitute applesauce for oil for a lighter, healthier recipe in the same way I can replace unhealthy energy vampires for more upbeat life builders. It's all part of the earth bowl, but I can choose to make life as healthy and tasty as possible.

*In the midst of an out of the blue anxiety attack, I write to remember that this fear won't physical hurt me but it can mentally kill me.

*Thank you: fresh idea about Plan A & B phases of an idea are "easier" than Plan M pieces. M represents Middle, in the Midst of an event. The Plan M stage is when the project becomes Most Mentally challenging. Right now, I don't have the Plan A-L stage of freshness and don't have Plan Z zone of victory, the end zone. Help me persevere.

*Thank you: seeing how more options can create chaos and restlessness. Sometimes the simple challenge of choosing right from wrong is enough of a choice. I crave variety and change, but lately it seems like general living has become complexly layered. Cell phone options, car models, clothes' styles, house layouts, job options. I'm on decision overload.

*Inspired to consider my 5 senses and list specific gratitude for each sense 7 days a week. Examples of thanks: Sight: to read fun blog; Taste: iced coffee with chocolate mint creamer; Smell: newly mopped floors; Touch: Luke's soft fur; Hearing: 80's music while I jump rope. This not only trains my mind for awareness, I'll have 35 reasons (plus!) to be grateful every week.

*Thank you: squirrels climbing trees by the pond. Through their behavior I see them as diligent workers collecting nuts, preparing for winter. They collect for possible lean times, but don't hoard. They take time to have fun as they playfully chase each other. Their claws are shod in peaceful reassurance without fear of slipping or jumping between trees. They don't sit at the end of one branch waiting for another squirrel to rescue them, prod them, or refer to a teaching manual about what order to jump on which limb. They simply take the next step or next lunge to handle what is necessary for that moment. Which of my natural squirrely instincts have been covered by fear or buried under excessive analysis? Lord, help me learn from the squirrels!

*Thank you: realizing how schools spend much effort and time preparing students for college. What would our graduating students look like if similar amounts of dedication and hours were spent preparing them for healthy dating, marriage choices, their walk with God?

*If I ever get asked to offer my best life giving advice, it would be to thrive on surprise. To surprise someone every day with a gift: a candy bar, a note, a song request dedicated on the radio, a phone call, a meal, a card. To stretch your creativity and know that by watering someone else's spirit with a surprise,

God will turn around and refill your watering can of life. I'll have seasons when I have more time. I'll have seasons when I have more money. In either season, I can surprise someone with at least one of these two commodities. To have life, I need to show life.

*Thank you: reminder that I am called to be light in a dark workplace. God doesn't put streetlamps in well-lit areas. Grow me to be like Paul who acknowledged a shipwreck but held tight to Your spiritual anchor!

*Thank you: witnessing Tig's style of living resembles a lot of Jesus' example: he uses few words, no rash judgment, gentle and caring without a strict personal pride agenda. He blends into crowds yet remains a solid and strong presence. Despite some of my verbal crucifixions, his spirit focuses on the resurrections of life. (This journal entry was from 11-16-14 after 20 + years of marital "practice.")

*Guard me against sloppy living. To accept where I am, what I have while balancing the wisdom to stretch as needed, rest as required.

*Thank you for this sweet priceless interaction!! Listening to Marley Mae play imagination travels with Tig. Hearing her say it was her turn to drive since Gramps drove last time and she was taking him to visit heaven. Tig asked how far it was to heaven and how would she know how to get there? She held up her color book drawing and said knew because she'd use that map. (Marley Mae was 3 when this journal entry was written).

*Thank you: recognizing the value, the need to think, be still. Sitting with You *is* being productive for what matters to You! The best use of my time is to sit at Your feet checking in for regular tune-ups, spiritual fuel and alignment.

*Thank you: real life example of seeing how my life represents the pen I'm using to write today. It's cheap, requires force to get a non-choppy look, struggle to push and pull vs. using a free flowing gel pen that glides across the page. I'm forcing and fixating to gain momentum vs. allowing the process of free flow of spirit. (I never imagined this journal entry would spark part of my book title!)

*Help me remember the heart and spirit are more important than saying the perfect words. Consistently meet people where they are. To praise rejoice, meet, cry, listen with them, not with anxiety that I'll say or not say the right thing.

*Thank you: a greater awareness of who You crafted me to be. If someone asked me today (12-6-14) what I'd fight for, I'd answer, "showing more gratitude means less hopelessness; more time to reflect means less blurry vision."

*Thank you: visual about the start of my quiet time resembling a shaken soda bottle. I need to settle completely before opening the top. Calm my spirit prior to opening any spoken thought or discussion!

*What would happen if everyone went back to handwriting their words instead of texting, typing, or using copy and paste? What if every word had to be handwritten before it could be spoken? A delightful visual that the world could be quieter, less harsh and more thoughtful.

*Thank you for Tig pointing out that when loved ones pass, they leave holes in our family and holes on earth. I'm grieving whole with a hole. Help me not to allow this healing gap determine my entire outlook. Slow motion is still motion. It may not be at the pace I'd like or the pace I'm used to, but it's still forward movement.

*Praise: quick catch in my spirit that when I feel tension while praying or thinking, it's because I'm focused on steering instead of allowing God to drive.

*Interesting how many people have a burning desire for variety. However when a restaurant alters their menu or a grocery store remodels, that spark for change becomes a snuffed out fire. How much do I really want a shake-up to 'same old' or 'break out of the monotony?'

*Necessary conviction! If a deployed soldier read the summary of my daily tensions, what would his or her perception of my day be? (written after I fussed that I had a 15 minute dog walking job when it was cold; a coaching session in a coffee shop that conversationally didn't flow; a late dr. appointment requiring me to fast all day)

*Entertaining thought: if a non-believer uses OMG, are they claiming that they are astonished by their God? Is OMG from someone who doesn't believe in God their first step in accepting Him?

*Grant me confidence to see other professionals as people to learn from, not compare myself to.

*Thank you: Your guidance in me needing to say "I'm sorry" only if there is injury or intentional offense. I've gotten into a habit of quickly apologizing as insurance to cover the possibility of letting someone down or not understanding something quick enough (according to me). To remember that it's ok to state healthy boundaries without fearfully assuming someone's disappointment. I respect others' boundaries but feel guilty for claiming needs that help me show up best for life.

*To make sure my prayers align with You! Guard me against treating God like a remote control. Guide me against lukewarm splashes and to really grasp the understanding of how much He love me even in my flightiness.

*Protect me against taking "once in awhile happenings" or isolated incidences and morphing them into "always and never."

*Nudge me to be like a cup of tea instead of a cup of coffee…to slowly steep for full flavor instead of being a burst of caffeine followed by an energy crash.

*To be content with viewing my first attempts as an opening to use resiliency and creativity to navigate to the next option. Why is it that I loved concocting new stories, using different colors, reading a variety of books when I was younger, but as an adult, play time developed into freak out time? Help me tap into imaginative scenarios with less rigid solutions!

*Protect me against discontent… wishing the world could go back to a primarily farming culture that set our lives around natural growing and hibernating seasons; where I saw contentment of animals and plants budding with the most basic needs; where life was based on light cycles, not a 24-7 clock. The sun-up to sun-down had light limits. Shopping malls, online business, and electronic connections disregard the need to have down time! Guard me against society's jaded lack of barriers that disrespect our Creator's plan.

*Thank you: recognizing how working toward internal peace and gentleness is similar to training for an ultra marathon. What am I feeding my mind (books, scripture, conversations, thoughts)? How am I disciplining my body daily (practice, cross train, form check, different courses)?

*Lord, I need you to take my hodge podge of thoughts and sort it out! Use this mud I bring and turn it into Your perfect mud mask. When You wipe away the mud bath of my mind, replace my toxic thoughts with Your reflective glow.

*Thank you: fun visual about multi-tasking on a heavily scheduled day. Worried that mixing my work-out with bible study wasn't reverent. Jesus is my friend and He's with me always no matter where I am. Just as fitness partners work out together, I can bring Jesus into every room of my heart. He's my fitness center, building my character core.

*Thank you: Waking to a new light. Anticipating what God's going to do vs. dreading what the world may do with this day. I enter today's terminal ready to fly. I can address yesterday's baggage, but I don't need to carry it on today's trip. Leave it at God's baggage claim to clean sweep and search its contents for possible hazards.

*Thank you: reality check that when I don't have streams of income ('current-sea?' ☺) , I have rivers of time. Let me use what I *have* to glorify You and Your plans for my life!

*Thank you: insight that over time, I've slowly bought the lie that martyrdom is status quo. That somehow if I was happy or filled with joy, I must be doing something wrong? Harsh to hear, but life giving to receive!

*Needing to soak in some fresh water! Align me with positive people, to absorb uplifting teachings. To drink from "well" water versus unfiltered worldly water! Feeling emotionally toxic and mentally polluted by today's abundance of sewer speakers in my path.

*Thank you: waking in the middle of the night with the word DO in my head. A double meaning to move and also an acronym for DO being Delayed Obedience. I've been called to write and that means now, not when I retire, when I have money, when I'm inspired, when my schedule is less full. Delayed obedience is disobedience.

*Thank you for fun creative thought, "If I give my first fruits of the day to writing, is that like having more concentrated juice? ☺

*Thank you: devotional teaching that our best life flow is not in the leisure times but rather when we're doing work that is using our highest ability; at moments when we're stretched yet time nearly vanishes because we're so caught up in that work that flows naturally from us.

*Thank you for finding Kelly Jull's *Tall Tree* book for golden nuggets: "If you can't make a sale, at least make a good impression," and "You cannot expect to have powerful positive influence over others if you are not in control of yourself."

*Thank you: learning to establish reasonable social outing boundaries, to invite assertiveness *and* gracious exit without guilt.

*Realizing how my oppression has been from being too much in my own head. Hearing in the spirit that I need to jump out of my thought barge and walk on water with God instead of sitting in my "thinking ship." Even in this season of gritty rocks, I still hunt His shiny diamonds in the desert sand.

*A flier advertised a 12 week skin-care rate that is more expensive than my 12 week life coaching rate. What makes people use money for external upgrades that will age or need to be rigorously maintained, yet hesitate to invest in their internal skin and soul care to produce fresh growth, wisdom, and revelation?

*To steep in the words from this morning's devotional: "When you feel unforgiven, question your feelings but don't question God. If our heart condemns us, God is greater than our heart." (1 Jn 3:20)

*Thank you: catching myself over thinking the past. It's ok to glance at the previous situation with a cursory review. Let that past be a learning tool, but not a hammer or a paddle!

*Praise for clarity to balance my perceptions with God's alignment. He places desires, passions in my heart and then stirs excitement as fuel to move. God gives me a fuel line but He is engine for His 20/20 vision. He has perfect foresight so before I hit the gas, I'm to check His map, gauges, timing belt. An extra praise because this visual provided laughter that makes me know how Tig's gear head style has rubbed off on me!

*Thank you: picturing me casting cares into an ocean using a rod and reel instead of bank fishing with a cane pole. Bank fishing allows me to see more of my own weaknesses. Casting with a rod and reel invites those cares to be further away from my immediate judgment and wishy-washy action. God's floods of revelation have surpassed my waves of pain.

*Tough lesson in quiet time…if I choose to be steadfast, I need to give God *everything*. If I choose to give nearly everything, that remaining 'almost everything' percentage becomes seed plant for the enemy's foothold. The enemy will multiply any percentage of whatever I don't fully vest in God. Eeks!

*Praise for Dad teaching me about Jesus' temperance. Jesus has energy and light but doesn't lead with mania and euphoria. Help me be wisely tempered!

*I've fallen into a trap of believing God responds the same way the world does. I've sadly adjusted to accept ring tone interruptions, distracted listening, and people overpowering the conversation with their own stories and figure this is what God does as well. I've distanced myself from God because I think He's weary from hearing the same thing or He prefers an abbreviated summary of my woes.

*When my patience runs thin, help me understand I can expect it but I don't have to accept it. Grow me to seek solutions to problems, to stop the complain drain! I've been like the Loony Tunes Taz stirring up dust and dirt in my mind and not even leaving a broom to sweep it up!

*Thank you: funny visual of mortal combat also like mental combat. I need to swat the simple house fly thoughts before they grows into something more like a horse fly or dragon fly!

*Reminder to pray *and* work. Soak with You, serve with others. Remind me to regularly claim I am God's day laborer, I am on His assigned payroll.

*Thank you: reality check about my stepping out of my own thoughts, running head first into a selfish block. When have I asked Jesus how HIS day is going? How often do I ask Jesus if HE wants my help or listening ear? Why don't I ask Him what HIS goals are for my life?

*Praise! Seeing how my crochet and pray method of meditation weaves peace into my soul. Transferring a ball of yarn turns my strands of nerves, thoughts, reflections into a productive pattern.

*Thank you for a funny visual in the shower about the current state of my soul needs a loofah made from 80 grit sandpaper! Take off the old caulk (thoughts) before I try to fill a new hole with fresh caulk.

Reminder to stop filling my internal gaps with gravel, dirt, sand just so that there isn't a soul hole.

*Thank you: Marley Mae's request for a hug when she needed comforting. She simply recognized her immediate need and asked for what she was lacking. Praise for learning from her innocence, seeing God's view of me as more adoring than the love I have for our granddaughter!

**Freshen my perception! Guide my eyes to see more of the chocolate pieces of life than the onion slabs stuck in my eyes.

*Protect me against over calculating life. Even though my weakness is math, by the amount of if/then geometric statements I wanted proven, you'd swear I was a math major! Help me flow vs. fixate!

*Eeks but smiling through conviction that I don't need *new* assignments, I need to develop and complete the *current* missions with excellence.

*Thank you for the humorous visual of spiritually armoring with my feet shod in peace but waiting for the other shoe to drop. Am I putting on flip flops or army boots for protection and peace?

THE BEST OF...

I began taking sermon notes in 2007 when we joined a church that encouraged writing reflections from the pastor's message. These written treasures have become my spiritual scrapbook. They are soul food for my heart to feast on. This collection is delivered in a non-standard editorial style and I'm reminded I'm blessed to live in an era of self-publishing. Like my journal musings, these are written in short form, hopefully with enough substance to understand, but with enough space to fill a reader's palate with what they extract from these sermon lessons.

Using a disclaimer from our church: every sermon contribution doesn't credit every source because pastors often use golden nuggets from writings or people. Evangelize God's word to others through others. If we're God's spokespeople, He's not concerned about who gets the credit for what is His anyway.

*Focus on God's presence, not the absence of your trouble.

*Satan tempts to destroy. God tests to develop. Do you want God's future potential or Satan's future pain? What is the lure that draws you or pulls you off track? Testing will produce perseverance. Temptation distances us from success.

*Are you correcting or connecting people? Are you willing to minister to hungry, unexpected, noisy, messy people or are you more concerned with your own agenda?

*Fellow church member sharing, "I'd rather have someone genuinely disinterested than falsely interested in what I say, do, or represent."

*Are you in chains? Shackled steps are stumbling steps. If we trust to scatter good seed, that scattered becomes gathered. Shackled hands can't and don't scatter. Bound givers can't and won't be bountiful givers.

*Beth Moore: "God isn't simply just a big us."

*Why choose failure when you can choose success? Invite a challenge to positively change you. Change only comes from challenges.

*While you're waiting for your dreams to come true, serve someone else's dream. Pour the gas of enthusiasm instead of marinating vinegar on someone else's dream. Life is a lesson of love using a crock pot recipe. Delays are part of the dream. God is never late, but also never early.

*From a *Touched by an Angel* clip: a reporter used crookedness to launch a jaded story. Angel Monica challenged the reporter's choice of integrity. He responded that he didn't have a choice to report the story if he wanted career advancement and to keep his job. She countered that we always have a choice. Sometimes we don't like a choice. Today's news quickly becomes tomorrow's history. We can choose to change tomorrow's news by what we do today. Angel Monica taught how our integrity fades gently but later that dimming truthfulness later becomes a harsh glaring light.

*What is your WOW factor? Weight Of Worship? Do you allow good enough or work toward great? Is your worship something or is it everything?

*From Stormie Omartian's book of devotions using Romans 3. Our faithlessness does not cancel God's faithfulness. We are to pray for those who we think don't deserve, don't believe, or don't think as we do. God doesn't judge, think, or believe as we do!

*God judges us by our compliance, not our performance. Are you changing or following God as you should? Changing and following both look like a continual growth, but pay close attention. Where is God saying woe? Be grateful for lack of surplus, emotional drain, or physical shortage. No reserves force us to cling and rely on God for everlasting change.

*Acceptance=standing in a long express lane checkout and being more aware of the people and surroundings than counting the basket items of the people in front of you.

*When the fear of change becomes less than the current pain, only then will we decide to do something differently! No change happens without a loss: loss of pride, loss of circumstances, loss of old heavy ways, loss of routine, loss of a person.

*Quit praying and start doing! Don't ask God for things that we know we are to do. Sometimes praying can be spiritual procrastination. Do we know more than what we practice? Often we know it, but don't do it. God gave us the book of Acts, not the book of ideas. He told us, "Well DONE, good and faithful servant." He didn't say, "Well *planned* good and faithful servant." He didn't say, "Well *thought* good and faithful servant" or "Well *prayed* good and faithful servant."

*What words describe your current prayer life? Do you find yourself digging into the garbage can of your mind and actions? Why would you stick your hand in the trash, much less pull out rubbish to review? God's time does not operate like clock time. Just because we spend one or two hours straight with God doesn't mean He got our full amount of time. How much time is spent in preoccupation, distraction, watching the time, mentally piddling through your day planner? God can do much with very little time if we are laser focused on Him!

*What are you proclaiming? Joy or simply false cheer? Joy is long term, false cheer is circumstantial. Focus on the anticipation of birth, not the pregnancy. When people visit a mother after a baby is born, concentrate on the baby's new life not the mother's pain.

*God loves drawing straight lines with crooked sticks...Matthew Kelly, *Resisting Happiness*.

*We know God's hand. We see His works, but do we know and seek His *face* and His *heart?*

*Rick Warren: Surrender is harder than fighting. Retirement isn't a Christian goal, it's a surrender to God's company. Surrender more, see more!

*Difficulties don't necessarily build character, they reveal character.

*Pastor Robert Morris: when someone begins gossip and then wants to draw you in, that's the enemy bait and reel tactic. Your best answer is to respond, "I don't know their heart like God does and I haven't walked their path."

*Vocation is defined as, "The place where God calls you is where your deep gladness and the world's deep hunger meet. Find that intersection and you will be filled with bubbling joy."

*Jeremy Camp's words of wisdom during an April 2016 concert: There is a universal struggle where we ask that x, y, and z are taken away from us. First, we need to give it to Him, lay it at His feet before He'll pick it up. How can we expect Him to take something that we won't use our free will to give Him?

*The more anger you have, the less control you have. Make an excuse or make a difference. It's your choice.

*Do your quiet times look more like a 10-15 minute one way phone conversation? The kind where you dial God, speed through your agenda, rattle off your needs and then hang up the phone and bolt out the door before He even gets to speak or answer?

*As your faith increases, your transformation will grow and your perspective of understanding will be wider. Study and live what you learned. Pick one Proverb a day and do that over and over until it grows into your core. Caution yourself against operating in a digital download delete with no action!

*Running from God is like running on a treadmill. You sweat, you're sore, you log miles, you're tired but in the end, once you jump off, you're still in the same place in the gym. What voices inside are calling you into hiding? Pull out those masks, sins, any wounds you're trying to cover, and then run *to* God with them. Those are the miles that count and will make greater impact on your spiritual marathon training.

*Count how many times in a single day you allow the enemy of defeat to knock at your heart's door. How often do you answer that door with a welcome sign? How many times do you greet the enemy of defeat by rolling out the red carpet and serving a plate of brownies? Who would pass up that invitation of hospitality?

*There is an intersection of tension when a need and a heart meet. People tend to give money easier because others may reject people but they won't reject cash. The fear you experience when you're out of your comfort zone is the pain from your faith growing. As your faith births, it becomes a labor pain. Whether it's a physical pregnancy or a spiritual rebirth, laboring includes contractions for that birthing process to be completed. Sometimes those contractions sound like can't, don't, or won't. The tightening of character muscles is designed as a way to encourage healthy birth versus a stillborn version of ourselves. Invite God to be your birthing Coach, your labor and delivery Doctor!

*Serve God with your heart, not your mind! We over think ourselves to the point of confusion. Since we can't figure out what God is doing, we fill our mind with something, anything so it makes sense to us. In heaven, we'll have eternity to *learn* the whys from living *out* the whys from our 80-90 years on earth.

*From a pastor's message *"Alice in Wonderland, Through a Looking Glass"*: Are you seeing backwards or as a direct reflection of who Jesus really is? Are we seeking His purpose or our preferences? Do any of us need barf bags for our heart because we spiritually vomit when we speak? Do a "gut" check! Does what you spiritually eat or drink grow you or diminish you? Watch your spiritual nourishment and remember that washed hands and washed hearts are soul purifiers.

*In dealing with doubts, remember that God isn't threatened by our questions. Earthly things create anxiety because they take our focus off our heavenly Father. When doubts arise, instead of asking what did *I* do or what *didn't* I do, ask God, what can You do? What will You do? The enemy may shoot bullets of doubt, but they're blanks. Paying attention to earth as your permanent home is like renting a hotel room and weeding the flower bed at the hotel. Concentrating on material gain is like renting a car and changing the rental's oil before you return it. It's not yours. You care, but only with a temporary focus. Our flesh and heart will fail, it's a passing part of the body, but God never fails!

*Keep your eyes up! Keep your eyes open! No more navel gazing if you really want to see all of Jesus.

*Think for a change. However you think, you are. That thought is what you become. You move in the direction of your strongest thought. Audit your thoughts and the worldly ones are going to be worry. The eternal ones will be peaceful. You mentally have explosive power to pull down strongholds. Use your dynamite and get out of your dungeon of deception. Dwell on excellence and practice it right away, no delay!

*Do not focus on small beginnings. King David started out as a shepherd then moved on to killing a lion, then a bear, then a giant. You only get the miraculous when you go through, not around, the mundane.

*Remember that waiting is an action because it requires the movement of discipline.

*How can we be content without growing complacent? Celebrate here vs. looking toward there. Appreciate the layovers without the obsessive destination disease.

*When we think we achieve on our own, we risk the comfort of no longer needing God. Remain desperate for Him because complacent cruise control leads to apathy and atrophy. Your challenge: what are you individually doing that is "over your head" that leaves you desperately praying for God to move? If your answer is nothing, then your prayers aren't currently big enough to require reliance on God. Develop and deploy your gifts.

*We are living in a real world watching an air brushed world. Intimacy has been replaced by adrenaline. Adrenaline touches the temporary body but intimacy touches the eternal soul.

*Drink from the cup of Redemption and Restoration! We are to fulfill our original intent for what God designed us to be and do. We've set our expectation and limit too low. Hell fears untapped potential so the enemy is always trying to derail your train and impede your progress. We waste money, time, and energy improving ourselves due to inferiority and insecurity. We are still seeing ourselves as slaves instead of cashing in on what God already bought for us through Jesus.

*God tests us to bless us; the devil tempts us to destroy us.

*From the series Bullet Proof: Our armor of God is like a bulletproof vest. You may get shot, it may hurt, but you won't die. We have pain, doubt, hurts, but Jesus took our bullet. When you doubt, picture Jesus showing you His hands and side to remind you that He left the Holy Spirit as our Comforter? Why would He have left us a Comforter if our lives were made to be comfortable? Doubt isn't what trips us up, it's fear and anxiety that rips us apart.

*People have gotten so touchy about talking about money that they'd find it easier to talk about sex. One member told Pastor he thinks people would have an easier time asking someone for sex than asking for money. Our tithe usually isn't a money issue, it's a heart issue.

*Your past is not your past if it's impacting your present. God knows your history, but He will rewrite your future. Do you like who you are becoming? With your answer, remember that our natural hardwire is to repeat the past because we do what we've seen.

*Everything that matters requires boldness. We don't have to pick up what the devil lies down.

*The enemy has authored a smash hit movie called *Paralyzed, Analyzed, Penalized: Our past, Present, and Future.* Get out of your mind's theatre playing any dark reels. Don't even pull them out of the bargain bin! They are not worth a nickel of your money or a minute of your time!

*Some people's idea about displaying their fruits of the spirit shows up as sour grapes!

*God doesn't pursue us for the present, He pursues us for a purpose. Be satisfied with *what* is your purpose vs. getting hung up on *when* will I live my purpose.

*Throw a grenade of gratitude. Launch thanksgiving in the middle of a negative battlefield. Misery travels in masses so it's best to sit with winners instead of whiners. The more you complain, the less you attain because you're focused on what you don't have (or what you think you should/need/deserve to have according to *you*)

*Grace is God giving us what we don't deserve. Mercy is withholding what we deserve, holding the intensity of the scolding. Jesus' example is love on steroids. He gives where He finds empty hands. Augustine taught, "Love God first and then you can do whatever you want." A poet wrote, "Love your crooked neighbor with your crooked heart."

*We have a love-hate relationship with water. We want rain but not a flood. Water was used to represent depression, anxiety, miracles and peace throughout the Bible. Noah's Ark, the healing pool, walking on water, storms, Jonah and the whale, the Red Sea, and baptism. Before God splits the water, you have to walk into it first. You can live without food for 30 days. You can only live without water for two days.

*Are you filling a sink hole with "er"? Thinner? Richer? Faster? Smarter? Bigger? Roomier? God cannot bless who you pretend to be. A me I see, a me I want to be. Who does God see?

*If you ever wonder if you have a pride issue, take this test. Look at your most recent group photo. Who do you look for first? The answer says it all.

I'm finishing this book with "the best of…" section last. It candidly ends with who we look at first in the picture. Through this ten year writing project, I see my reflection in a wide variety of mirrors. Some mirrors are smudged, some are crystal clear, some are sized-to-fit, others are distorted, all represent some part of myself. That's the only person I can claim. I admire reflections of other people, but at the end of a day or the end of this book, my face and my name belong to that mirror image. I am made in God's image. John 1:12 tells me I am God's child. Romans 8:35-39 reassures me that I cannot be separated from the love of God. God is responsible for me, I am responsible to Him. I am confident that the good work God has begun in me will be perfected (Phil 1:6).

FORWARD!

Traditionally, a book foreword is written at the beginning of a manuscript. I write mine at the end, with hindsight and foresight wrapped into one efficient package.

I know this chapter is the last woven square in my patchwork of stories. It's a colorful crazy quilt pieced together with humor and lessons I've learned from life. It represents a collection of rich blessings from others sewing and sowing into me.

I leave this book with much to say intersecting with nothing more to say. It is complete as is. The quilt blocks are not seamless. There are stains, bleach spots, and ripped stitches. It is a written covering to collectively wrap my head around a compilation of thoughts.

Ironically, it started to rain as I finished that sentence about a covering. This book is an umbrella, an awning. It's life as I knew it in 2008 and life as I know it in 2018. I expected to publish this book much sooner. I intended to write a lighthearted whimsical potpourri of randomness. Instead the finished piece turned into a decade of wisdom that I hadn't run out to find in my original quest to write a "just because" book. I pray that each reader will gain at least one valuable nugget to unlock their internal treasure chest.

I'm humming *"Don't Take the Girl"* by Tim McGraw. That song leaves the conclusion to the listener's discretion about the girl's fate. It subliminally harmonizes with my stage of life from aspiring childhood author to dating to marriage to pregnancy. Our parenting experience includes a child who is a musical author. Where will his songs lead him?

I passionately flirted with my writing love, but spent years dating other employer-based relationships in case my first love didn't work out. Through a series of intensive desert assignments, I face planted in abrasive sand and allowed the camel herds to trample me. I existed through everyone else's written job description, allowed myself to be pigeon holed because it made sense to their mission. I'm picking cactus needles from my teeth and reapplying intensive aloe lotion to the road rash on my heart. I walk forward with SPF sun block, feet shod in peace. This time I lace up mountain climbing boots instead of slipping on flip flops.

A marriage between author and writing will transpire in several wedding chapels, publishing venues. I'm faithfully pursuing work I love and believe our love will conceptualize into multiple births. I will spring forth *the* life that crafted into my DNA. This book ends as a mystery that doesn't need or want to be solved. Each day provides clues toward my proclamation at The Pinnacle. I have supporting evidence through map markers and Promises to lead to new passageways and revelations. As a daughter of the Creator of the World, I am the head, not the tail (Dt. 28:13). I have not been given a spirit of fear, but of power, love, and a sound mind (2 Tim 1:7). I have been chosen and appointed to bear fruit (Jn. 15:16).

In 2008, to the logical business world, I physically appeared to be stronger overall. In 2018, I am mentally and spiritually more anchored in a cove that doesn't neatly fit into a materially packaged world. I am the girl running off to elope with what engages her heart and makes it "marry" (pun intended).

God has tremendous things planned for me. I walk through this open door wearing sunglasses for a bright future, not with blinders to shield me from the past. You have journeyed through my wedding album, parts of my history book.

With some desert sand still residing in my teeth, I expect those gritty granules to transform into freshwater pearls of perception. I resolve not to allow a temporary face plant in a desert to produce continual harvest and re-seed in that arid ground. So…with a country music hymnal in my head, I graduate to the next level of writing with *Don't Take the Girl* on repeat play. I commission myself with *The Dance* by Garth Brooks. I could have missed the pain, but I'd have had to miss the dance.

I have much to learn, much to live. I'm grateful that I leave this book knowing that life's too short for dull razors, cheap pens, and worn out underwear.

Life's Too Short for Dull Razors, Cheap Pens, and Worn Out Underwear | Christina Eder

www.ingramcontent.com/pod-product-compliance
Lightning Source LLC
Chambersburg PA
CBHW071311110526
44591CB00010B/860